GARY LANG

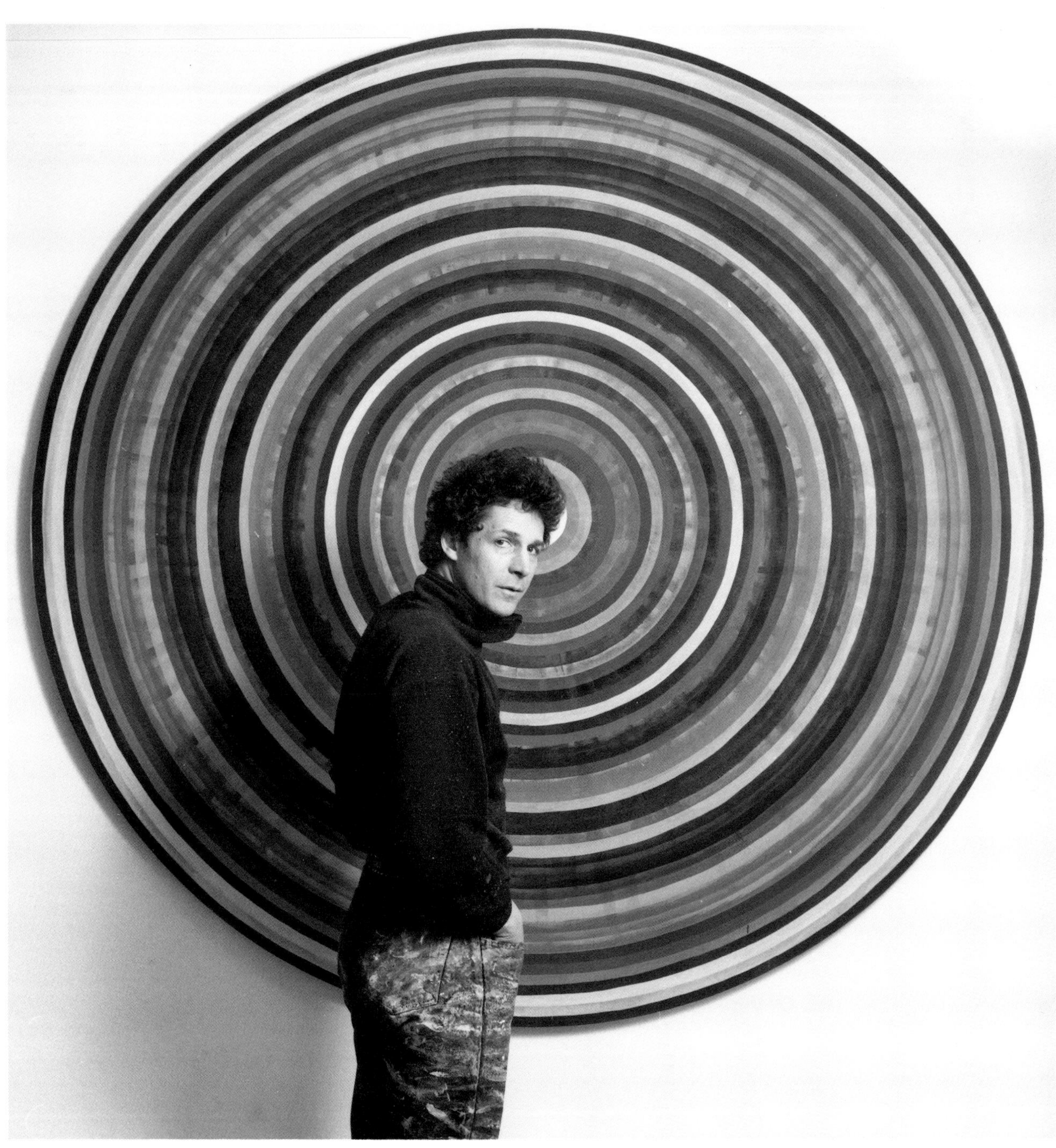

GARY LANG
PAINTINGS AND OBJECTS
1975–1997

Essays by
Stanley I Grand
Susan C. Larsen
Appreciation by
James Turrell

May 11–August 10, 1997

Sordoni Art Gallery
Wilkes University
Wilkes-Barre, Pennsylvania

Text Copyright © 1997 Sordoni Art Gallery
Illustrations Copyright © 1997 Gary Lang
Photograph of Gary Lang, page 2, Copyright © 1995 Sebastiano Piras, New York

2000 copies were printed
by Llewellyn & McKane Inc., Wilkes-Barre, Pennsylvania

Catalogue design by John Beck
Color photographs by Ken Showell
Cover photographs by Bill Orcutt and Ilonka Van Der Putten

Set in the Adobe issue of Monotype Centaur,
a typeface designed in 1915 by Bruce Rogers.

ISBN 0-942945-10-7

Cover painting
Mirroring Heart (Banding), 1993–97
acrylic on canvas
113 × 113 inches
Detail on front

G ARY LANG is a treasured friend. His personal history includes a religious conviction that speaks to his chosen vision. He makes paintings with as much a detailed and layered history of where he has been as they are the singular and sweeping vision of where he has arrived. The works explore continents in the world of visual thought. They are to be entered.

James Turrell

WOVEN INFORMATION

Stanley I Grand
Wilkes University

AMONG THE ARTISTS who received recognition in the 1980s, Gary Lang is a special case. Never gaining superstar status during the years when fame came quickly and departed even more so, Lang has earned the respect of his peers and the esteem of a knowledgeable group of collectors and critics. This mid-career survey seeks to understand the nature of his accomplishment by establishing a chronology and contextualization of his works, by providing an interpretation of his philosophy and a decoding of his methodology, and by locating him within the context of the great modernist colorists from Cézanne to Josef Albers. Despite, or rather precisely because of, Lang's initially startling palette and the often radical appearance of his paintings, he is best understood as a classic painter, a true scion of the modernist tradition in which he has both respectfully dwelt and advanced.

After receiving his M.F.A. from Yale in 1975, Lang moved to Barcelona, where he spent two years on a Fulbright scholarship. In the northeastern Spanish city so closely identified with Antoni Gaudí, Lang's work underwent a change. Perhaps not coincidentally, much of Lang's work from this period combines humor (Gaudí's *Casa Milá* [1905–07] is the quintessential comic-book apartment house) and ascension (Gaudí's *Sagrada Familia* [begun 1884] comes to mind). Earlier, as a graduate student, he had made "paintings about frontality and ascension that looked like Don Judd sculptures done in a Day-Glo and glitter palette."[1] Now, fascinated with and inspired by the bright, animated, and colorful bits of paper that he encountered constantly and collected avidly, Lang began to move away from a formalist, fluorescing minimalism toward collage.

The earliest work in this exhibition, *Barcelona Painting* [Figure 1], is an icon in which paper scrap information has been translated into a painted collage. Employing a vertical format, the painting reads like a scroll or totem pole, with each course providing a different level of information. According to Lang, he "was accumulating and assembling cultural refuse and recycling it into energized totems, spiritual batteries, with intensely charged force-fields."

Reading the painting in an ascending manner, one sees, in the lower quarter, a noncanonical Mickey Mouse, with a nose reminiscent of W.C. Fields's red proboscis, striding into the picture from the left along a lightning bolt. Not only does the lightning form a pathway through the flames rising from the curvature of a celestial orb, but it also strikes a fantastic, trucking space vehicle—designed no doubt by R. Crumb—approaching from the opposite direction. Multicolored planets are scattered across the firmament; and a baroque cartouche, empty of script, dangles from a spiky envelope that contains an indecipherable inscription. Surrounding and framing the spacewalker are three patterned panels: on the top, seven parallel lines; on the left, arcs of blue and white orbiting a yellow mass; and on the right, a plaid-like design of intersecting lines. The ensuing layer of information contains brightly colored intersecting blades of yellow, blue, and red that reference a scrap of paper Lang brought back from a visit to Morocco. The abstracted Arabic script recalls its place of origin. To the left is an upside-down fragment of an old-fashioned, romantic postcard decorated with hearts and flowers that once proclaimed that separation tears the heart asunder. To the right is a miniature still-life arrangement consisting of a pair of cherries, a lemon, and a strawberry. Although these fruits evoke the slot machine's wheels of chance, they were in fact appropriated from a tea bag marketed by a German firm under the *Fixbute* label.

The next stratum juxtaposes a classical goddess with contemporary action superheroes. On the right, set in a yellow triangle, is a figure descended from the Venus de Milo. The adaptation, however, is clearly more commercial than æsthetic; we are looking at the logo for Venus noodles, beans, or some such product. Beneath, red letters appear to spell out *Jazz*. The triangle cuts into flat stripes of alternating blue and white. To the left, a daringly foreshortened Captain America, the Marvel Comics hero, swings away from a pair of nefarious villains, one of whom wears a patch over his right eye. The outcome of his escape remains uncertain: as the embodiment of America soars past a balcony, another figure, dressed in green, reaches up to grab him.

Softening the upward and outward momentum created in the lower panels, an image of a brightly colored tropical fish swims through progressively lightening layers of brown pigment. This image, derived from a postage stamp, is pasted atop a horizontal cartoon panel, a pop descendent of the isocephalic classical frieze. Above and to the left, a white, biomorphic form—an orchid or hand perhaps—in a field of pink is followed by the mottled trunk of an upside down birch tree that springs from loopy, almost Burchfield-like grass. In the upper right corner, the Hindu god Siva (Shiva), in blue, wearing a red headdress and a flower lei, raises a flute to his lips and serenades the object of his ardor, who holds a lei as well. Covering her legs and thighs, a long, blue dress, whose folds appear like Ionic fluting, falls to the ground. Above them is a dramatic, pink-hued sky; at their feet, a lush lawn where a duck and peacock (a traditional symbol of pride) are standing. In the midst of this idyllic, pastoral scene of tender love, a caricature of the square-jawed, virile American male, whose ancestors include the Marlboro man, incongruously appears.

Combining images from a variety of sources and cultures, this brassy, cacophonic painting should be understood as an allegory of creation, destruction, and the conflict between good and evil. Lang's utilization of images from popular and mass culture, however, serves as an ironic antidote to the pretensions of high art and allegorical seriousness while nonetheless affirming his commitment to these values. In his seminal work, *Allegory: The Theory of a Symbolic Mode*, Angus Fletcher noted that "In the simplest terms, allegory says one thing and means another."[2] Continuing, he writes that as a "mode: it is a fundamental process of encoding our speech."[3] Frequently, as in Dante's *Commedia* or John Bunyan's *The Pilgrim's Progress*, the allegory takes the form of a journey or quest in which the protagonist confronts choices, adversities, and hardships. In *Barcelona Painting*, allegory takes the form of an encoded quest in which the artist, incarnated as an intoxicated mouse, travels between flames and void along the narrow lightning bolt of inspiration in pursuit of a new vision. Art, the painter seems to say, has the power to intoxicate, to induce ecstacy (*ekstasis*, to stand out of place), to move one into another realm. In this case the journey winds through the realms of popular culture and high art, nature and religion, love—whether sentimental, erotic, or spiritual—and conflict. The simultaneity of the cycle of creation–destruction is suggested by the presence of Siva, who—along with Brahma (the Creator) and Vishnu (the Preserver)—forms the Hindu *Trimurti*. In this case, however, Siva appears not as the Trimurti Destroyer but as a generative or procreative force, with the flute recalling both the linga and Siva's patronage of the arts, especially dancing. This polarity also appears in the juxtaposition of the threatened Captain America with the threatening "Marlboro Man," who aggressively intrudes into the top panel. In *Barcelona Painting* creativity and destruction weave together like an electrical charge oscillating between the positive and negative poles in a storage battery. Like a Shakespearean fool, irony serves to undermine the distinction between the serious and the banal; nonetheless, the painting expresses a gravity of intention that is found throughout Lang's work.

Although Lang loved Barcelona, his work was as out of place there as it had been in New Haven. When he showed his paintings at the Institute of North American Studies "people didn't know what to make of them . . . because at that time in Barcelona it was still burlap and bull's blood and earth. Tàpies. That was it."

Lang's return to America in 1976 initiated a decade-long period of struggle. After settling in New York, where he painted until 1979, he moved to Los Angeles to be closer to his father who was very ill. In order to support himself, Lang worked full time in an electric supply warehouse. At night, often too tired to paint, he channeled his pent-up energies into *Weapons* [Figures 2a & 2b], objects of woven aluminum and rubber. These disturbing, spiky objects evoke a nether world—explored by other artists including Nancy Grossman, Robert Mapplethorpe, and Nan Goldin—of leather, dildos, and blackjacks; a sadomasochistic world where the line between violence and pleasure has blurred. But they also work as shamanistic fetishes like the nail-studded power figures from Zaire. Concerning these works, Lang has noted the contradiction between their creation and their appearance: "Although they have a menacing, brutal look, the process of weaving and wrapping is calming and quiet. I called them *Weapons* because that is what they are. I think of all my work as an invasive vehicle that attacks and shatters the mundane." Despite his critical success with the *Weapons*, Lang felt the necessity to go beyond them: "People will respond to something, but you have to keep moving in order to keep from plagiarizing yourself." Gradually, the wrapped objects assumed a less sinister quality as in *Urn* [Figure 5a]. These in turn led "to larger minimal looking objects which I called *Bullets*" [Figure 5b]. Indeed, throughout the early 1980s, Lang worked in a variety of different modes simultaneously as he alternated between works that combined images, such as the stapled aggraphages [Figure 6], and paintings such as *Dried in Sound* [Figure 3] or *Isn't It Wonderful* [Figure 4].

In 1984 Lang's father died, and his marriage began to unravel. He responded to these events with a frantic creative outburst. Looking back he recalls that between 1985 and 1988 he created "more paintings than at any time in my life—I was painting all night and all day. The paintings were going in a variety of directions." Returning to New York in 1985, Lang supported himself as a maître d' at the Limelight, a popular Manhattan club. As keeper of the velvet rope, he became one of those judges, like Osiris, who determined who could gain entry to the modern mystery religion known as the downtown club scene. Nor was he able to escape its often self-destructive lifestyle. The violence done to individuals' self-images (as well as the physical threats that came from the excluded—Lang recalls numerous occasions when he found himself on the wrong end of a handgun) is summarized in *Night Life* [Figure 8].

One of Lang's most ambitious paintings to date, *Night Life* combines bursts of staccato pattern and amplified imagery to create a simultaneously joyful and menacing vision. Emerging from an active field of rectangles and squares is a sinister cyclopean figure with a "head" composed of one Rubik's cube set into another. The "eye," a red pixie derived from the White Rock logo, bends over a still pool and gazes at her reflection like Narcissus (whom Leon Battista Alberti, in *Della Pittura* [1435–1436], called the first artist). Surrounding the pixie are animation lines, a device that Keith Haring also adopted from the world of comics. Beneath the head, nine revolver barrels imperil the viewer. You stare, disbelievingly, at the stubby pistol fanning across your chest in the slo-mo, stop-action sequence of a nightmare before it comes to rest directly opposite your heart: Hell's Kitchen Futurism. Although the revolver recalls images as diverse as Andy Warhol's *Triple Elvis*, 1962, or the famous Army recruiting poster that proclaims "Uncle Sam Wants You," the source is actually a paper target, used by various police departments, that depicts a pistol-packing, Dick Tracy–type thug. By rendering the gunman's clothing in red, white, and blue, Lang seems to be implying a more ominous reading of the assailant as a renegade Captain America.

In *Night Life*, we see the entire range of Lang's subsequent formal vocabulary: the intersecting lines, early stars (*Arsenal of Stars for Chance* [Figure 24]), and dots (*Prayers* [Figure 15]). Along the lower edge, the painted pattern recalls works like *Isn't It Wonderful* [Figure 4]. Lang's fascination with Mexican textiles, which he collects, is apparent in the lines of bright color that appear alongside the pixie. Most interesting, in light of his subsequent work, are the careful, academic studies of color shifts along the sides of the Rubik's cubes. If one disregards Lang's neo-pointillist color sprinkles, the experiments of Josef Albers come to mind unbidden.

Despite the raw voltage of the images derived from the detritus of contemporary civilization, Lang began to feel that the true, expressive "power of the painting was coming from the grounds." In large part this was a consequence of a growing self-awareness that "the emphasis in my *process* was not on rendering the image, but on energizing the surface." This led to an alternate, more direct "method for ordering the chaos," one in which "the colors themselves became the subject matter." Transcending the need to think about pictorial subject matter and returning to his reductive, minimalist roots, he found that by focusing exclusively on painting lines of color, he could infuse his paintings with "more energy, more life, and more content because, if you eliminate imagery, the surface itself must speak for you."

Foo Lion [Figure 9] is a key work in Lang's transition from paintings that incorporated imagery to those that deal primarily with "energizing surfaces." By allowing the object, that is the lion, to act as the image, Lang was able to concentrate on the surface, which he activated with a spiky aura and a painted skin. In retrospect he realizes that "it wasn't the form I was seeking out, but rather a surface to paint." *Foo Lion* thus synthesized and summarized several strands of development explored previously in painted objects such as *Urn* [Figure 5a], the hand-held *Weapons* [Figures 2a and 2b], and paintings such as *Night Life* [Figure 8]. Thereafter, having abandoned overt subject matter and committed himself to the painting of lines, Lang found his artistic voice. No longer "concerned with making a painting," Lang rediscovered the "pure pleasure of direct painting" in the process of "weaving colors."

Begun in 1987, the "plaid paintings" were an early manifestation of this new direction. (Their antecedents, as we have seen, go back as early as *Barcelona Painting*.) Although misinterpreted initially ("Colleagues thought I was making crosses or grid paintings, but I was never interested in, or excited by, the grid"), Lang viewed them metaphorically as "an accumulation of intersections or crossroads." Describing the creation of *Plaid Painting* [Figure 12], Lang said "Using a very thin paint, I'd make just one brushstroke from the top to the bottom of the rectangular canvas. Then I'd rotate the canvas ninety degrees and paint another line from top to bottom, continuing in this way until the canvas was finished." In these works, it "wasn't what I was painting or even what the painting looked like, but rather the way I painted."

Subsequently, Lang ceased painting the lines freehand and employed tape to make his lines. Tape, which he had used previously to construct objects such as *Weapon* or *Urn*, now was used to delineate hard-edge lines of color in works such as *Ruth's Truths* [Figure 17]. The resulting paintings tended to be "aggressive because an abrupt hard edge is created when you pull the tape off." Unlike the "tender" gesture of "delicately dragging a bead of paint down a canvas," tape produces a "different sensibility. Everything about it—the crisp hard edge, the sound of the tape ripping off—is sharp, curt, and angular. It's like steel." But the tape also allowed for a thicker, denser application of color: "You can trowel in pigment in a way that you couldn't paint it on; if you tried to paint it on that thickly, it would just fall down." (Lang's fascination with tape came to full fruition in The Hague project, where he constructed the image entirely of woven colored tape.[4])

Lang's rediscovery of the "pure pleasure" of creating art coincided with several other changes in his life. After completing *Night Life*, he quit the club scene. In 1990, he met Ruth Pastine, a painter, whom he subsequently married. With this positive influence in his life, calmness displaced the frantic, frenetic energy that had informed his work. He has stated, "When I met Ruth something happened: the work began to change—to become more open, adventurous, and intimate." At about this same time he began painting mirrors and circles, two avenues of discovery that he has continued to pursue throughout the 1990s.

The first *Mirror* had a most unlikely genesis. Lang recalls "taking a shower and looking into a convex mirror that I kept in the stall. Up close I could see every pore in my face, but when I held the mirror at a distance, I saw a luminous, 3-D square." The quality and depth of the light reminded him of a cloudburst experienced in the Caribbean: "the way rain just sort of floats through the air, instead of falling straight down and pounding off the pavement as it does in the city. The *Mirrors*, which are soft and ethereal, are like clouds of droplets blowing in the breeze and reflecting the entire color spectrum." This sense of sparkling, watery prisms drifting across a field describes the effect of the *Mirrors* [Figures 16 and 20], where colors shift and metamorphose, as they dance across the surface of the painting, first embracing then abandoning, the radiant, contradictory light.

By blurring distinctions between viewer, object, and artist, the mirror serves as a vehicle for meditation or self-discovery: "I think of the mirror as I'm looking at you and I'm seeing myself since so much of what we see is a projection of ourselves." This concept of the mirror as pathway to knowledge has a long pedigree in Western art and mythology. Like the apple in the Garden of Eden, it can represent forbidden knowledge: Ovid (*Metamorphoses* 3:347–349) recounts how the blind seer Tiresias warned Liriope that her son Narcissus would live to a ripe old age only if he never came to know himself. Unfortunately, Narcissus gazed upon his own reflection in the mirror surface of a still pool and thus sealed his fate. In classical times, the mirror was an attribute of Venus. In Renaissance and Baroque art, the mirror was often associated with the minor vice of vanity. An outstanding example is Velázquez's *Venus and Cupid* (1648–1651, the "Rokeby Venus" now in the National Gallery, London) in which a sensual, recumbent nude stares into a mirror held by a putto. The presence of a mirror also serves to identify several allegorical figures including Prudence, Truth, and Time. In Old Master *vanitas* paintings, those reminders that death is ever stalking, a beautiful young woman often looks into her mirror and sees the visage of an old crone. This conceit continues to attract artists; one thinks of George Tooker's various *Mirrors*, for example. Finally, and without exhausting the topic, the *Speculum sine macula*, the flawless mirror, which Solomon had evoked in his praise of wisdom (Wisdom 7:26), became one of the signifiers of Mary's virginity and purity.

The second avenue of discovery, the concentric circle [Figures 13 and 23], is as richly encoded as the *Mirrors*. For Lang, it provides a means of "weaving the maximum random potential into a profoundly simple geometric format." (For the past several years, Lang has confined himself to painting two geometric shapes: squares [one thinks again of Albers] and circles [Vasari reminds us that Giotto knew that a perfect, handdrawn circle was both "enough and too much" of a gift for Pope Benedict].)[5] The circle, moreover, is simultaneously (1) self-referential (recalling Lang's years as a warehouseman in Los Angeles, his wrapped works, and his multitude of painted objects); (2) reflective of certain contemporary modes (the *Target* paintings of Jasper Johns or Kenneth Noland for example); and (3) evocative of the art-historical tradition (among other works, it has an obvious relationship with Giovanni di Paolo's *The Creation and The Expulsion of Adam and Eve from Paradise*, c. 1445, in the Metropolitan Museum of Art).

Indeed the tondo, as the Italians call the circular format, has a deep pool of associations that can only be hinted at in a short essay. Concentric rings represent both an earlier model of the heavens, as charted by the astronomer Ptolemy, and a road map of hell, as followed by Dante and his guide Virgil. Later, in the Renaissance, the circle and the sphere (a circle in three-dimensions) were considered perfect shapes, symbolizing Marsilio Ficino's Neo-Platonic conception of the universe as an hierarchical orb consisting of the Cosmic Mind (*mens mundana*), Cosmic Soul (*anima mundana*), spirit (*spiritus mundanus*), and matter (*materia*) arrayed in descending concentric levels. According to Erwin Panofsky "An uninterrupted current of supernatural energy flows from above to below and reverts from below to above, thus forming a *circuitus spiritualis*, to quote Ficino's favourite expression."[6] This same movement of energy occurs in a Gary Lang tondo. The circle is also an ancient symbol of the cycles, whether of life, the seasons, or fate. In Baroque allegorical representations, Human Life always stands on Fortuna's Wheel, reminding all that periods of ascension are soon followed by those of decline.

The circle symbolizing change is key to understanding Lang's tondi because the format is "a metaphor for what I've learned from nature. I love weather, its unpredictability and changing nature, which is as close to the truth as I've ever gotten." Noting that "I have most of the images and films of tornados," he adds "I find them beautiful as well as terrifying. Moving in a line, ascending and descending centrifugally, the tornado changes everything in its path. It's an important metaphor." Indeed, it takes little imagination to view the conical form of the brightly painted, aqua and cerise *Bullet* [Figure 5b], with its spiraling rings, as an inverted tornado. From the *Barcelona Painting* and the *Weapons*, this image of the destroyer as creator has been a constant in Lang's artistic vocabulary. But the tondi, recalling rainbows, also carry a mixed promise of benevolence (Genesis 9:12–16. The Hebrew *qešet*, which is used in Genesis 9:13 to mean (rain)bow, appears elsewhere in the Bible as the common word for *bow*, the weapon used to propel an arrow. *Qešet*, therefore, is simultaneously a sign of the Covenant, representing a Self-disarming of the Deity, as well as the powerful instrument that hurls His lightning-bolt arrows of destruction. Lang's assertion, quoted earlier, that all his work is a weapon, seems particularly apt in this context.)

Since 1990, when Lang painted the first of his concentric *Circles* on the wooden end-piece of an "old discarded wire-cable" spool, he has developed a complex mathematical system for ordering and selecting his palette. In the *Circles* [Figures 13 and 23] he weaves together a fixed palette and a mutating palette according to a working drawing or "navigational chart." After completing his navigational chart, which is a series of ratios between the fixed and mutating palettes, Lang works quickly and intuitively to select his fixed palette from hundreds of containers of mixed colors. He then picks his single mutating color.

Having chosen the initial colors of the fixed "random" palette, Lang starts a tondo at the outer edge by painting a concentric circle with the first color selected. (Previously, Lang had underpainted the canvas with large alternating rings.) Next he uses the second color and continues painting concentric circles until all the colors have been used. Then he paints a circle in his mutating color before selecting the next group of colors in his fixed palette (he never repeats a color). Once he has finished painting the second group of fixed colors, he alters the mutating color by mixing in an additional color or colors. Every time his working drawing calls for a concentric circle in a mutating color, he changes the hue by adding or subtracting colors. Thus if the mutating color starts out as an orange or pink, it might move first toward black and then toward white or red or blue until he decides to turn it in another direction. This process continues until the final circle, in the center of the tondo, has been painted.

Staring at the *Grand Circle* [Figure 23], one feels almost mesmerized (recall that Dr. Mesmer used a small disk to hypnotize his patients). The push-and-pull movement caused by the color shifts in this overwhelming painting—its diameter is more than twice the height of the average individual—virtually sucks you in like a vortex or whirlpool: "it defies you, dresses you down to your essential self, and refigures you. It's easy to get lost in this pictorial space, and some individuals become almost nauseous while looking at the painting. The goal is to reorient oneself via disorientation." One only feels this orientation–disorientation in the presence of the painting; reproductions never convey the impact of Lang's paintings: "When people say they don't get anything from my slides, I understand; it's not the slides, it's the paint, the surface, that records the human touch. The power of a painting is unleashed when you're in its presence." The mark, the artist's touch, is what animates Lang's paintings: the "touch is alive." Thus "the surface of the painting is the subject matter. The surface is what's talking to you on a primal level; that's what's affecting your body and your perceptual apparatus. In other words, the subject matter is the painting itself."

While weaving together color systems according to his numeric code, Lang varies the width of each concentric circle intuitively, responding both to the interaction of the colors and to their modification by the underpainting. The result of this "codi-fied improvisation," which Lang compares to jazz, is a maximization of the potentiali-ties of intuition and chance, with the goal of creating new color configurations and experiences.

Colors are the means by which Lang investigates the unknown. Although highly verbal, Lang, a self-described "color addict," has observed that "I'm more confident with colors because I feel connected to them." Nonetheless while at Yale, Lang had made a special point of avoiding Josef Albers ("a real color scientist") and his color theories: "I did not read that book [*Interaction of Color*] because I didn't want to intellec-tualize my knowledge about colors." Still, had Lang read Albers's book, he would have found ample support for his own experiments. Lang is doing intuitively what Albers was doing scientifically, and the results are the same, as Lang has acknowledged obliquely: "In the end, Albers used color to get you to float and vibrate. . . . He was walking a line between spirit and science, and in this way we are linked."

Josef Albers had argued that "preferences and dislikes—as in life so with color—usually result from prejudices, from lack of experience and insight."[7] Rather than accepting a limited palette, Albers advocated a broad embracement of the chro-matic scale: "Therefore, we try to recognize our preferences and our aversions—what colors dominate in our work; what colors, on the other hand, are rejected, disliked, or of no appeal. Usually a special effort in using disliked colors ends with our falling in love with them."[8] Moreover, a point that refers specifically to Lang's way of working, Albers had recognized that "independent of harmony rules, any color 'goes' or 'works' with any other color, presupposing that their quantities are appropriate."[9] (Lang: "People would say these colors don't go together, but in life everything is thrown together.") The appropriate quantities are determined by two factors: "how much and how often, distinguish 2 kinds of quantity: 1 of size—extension in area—and 1 of recurrence—extension in number."[10] Like Lang, Albers recognized that "By giving up preference for harmony, we accept dissonance to be as desirable as consonance. . . . Besides a balance through color harmony, which is comparable to symmetry, there is equilibrium possible between color tensions, related to a more dynamic asymmetry."[11] Albers also observed that painting lines was an excellent way to create works "in which color exists for color's sake . . . and not merely as accompaniment to form, to shape. . . . By combining colors exclusively in stripes—that is, in stretched, narrow rectangles, all of the same length, varying only in width, and touching each other in full length—we are led to overlook their rather equal shapes and to consider them almost shapeless."[12] Lang's aim, however, is not to investigate color combinations. Rather it is to transmit "essential information by means of an emotional code."

Ultimately, Lang believes that his art is "a spiritual conduit," but he distin-guishes between religion and spirit: "At one time, spirit and religion were unified; but spirit and religion are not the same anymore. There is a spirit, a living spirit, and that's the wellspring source of my work." He defines this living spirit as "the essential feeling one feels about being alive. What I'm sharing through my work is my feeling for life. That's what I have to offer. That is what fuels my efforts." Art is a means to transcend the boundaries between individuals: "It's a way to bridge, connect, and bond your spirit to someone else's. Ultimately, you're trying to connect your feeling for life with others'." Lang's feeling and enthusiasm for life are apparent in his sense of generosity: "Maybe the essential spirit of the work is abundance." Indeed one of the aphorisms that Lang likes to repeat is "All that is not given is lost."

In the final analysis, what Lang gives the viewer is a paradigm for organizing chaos, for infusing meaning into randomness. Indeed, it is this drive that separates the twice-wise hominid (*homo sapiens sapiens*) from other species. That is what we do. Like the scientist (Lang's interwoven colors and wrapped objects, ascending in a spiral motion, do not seem altogether foreign from the Watson–Crick model of DNA), priest, writer, philosopher, administrator, or any other individual, Lang seeks to make sense out of and understand the series of random acts against which we live our brief lives. "What am I really doing in these paintings? It occurred to me while working in my studio that I could 'start somewhere and go nowhere.' I was struck by this and immediately wrote it down. In the same moment, I realized that the truth is you 'start nowhere and go somewhere.' Where does anything begin? It begins where it begins. Change is the constant. There is nothing to hold on to. If you can embrace this, you can live. That is the essence of my work."

NOTES

1. All quotations are from a conversation with the author on December 18, 1996.
2. Angus Fletcher, *Allegory: The Theory of a Symbolic Mode* (Ithaca: Cornell Paperbacks, 1970): 2.
3. Ibid., p. 3.
4. The piece measured 134 × 134 inches and was created directly on the wall.
5. Giorgio Vasari, *Lives of the Artists*, ed. and trans by E. L. Seely (New York: Noonday Press, 1957): 8.
6. Erwin Panofsky, *Studies in Iconology: Humanistic Themes in the Art of the Renaissance* (New York: Harper & Row, Icon Editions, 1972): 132.
7. Josef Albers, *Interaction of Color*, paperbound ed. (New Haven: Yale University Press, 1971): 48.
8. Ibid., p. 17.
9. Ibid., p. 44.
10. Ibid., p. 43.
11. Ibid., p. 42.
12. Ibid., pp. 47–49.

TRACKING THE HEART'S OWN INTUITION

Susan C. Larsen
Chief Curator, Farnsworth Art Museum, Rockland, Maine

ONE OF THE RARE PLEASURES of a life lived in the artistic community is that of following the progress of a major painter from early promise through fascinating stages of development to a state of completeness and fulfillment. Viewed in retrospect, the artistic evolution of Gary Lang, from 1975 to today, has been a brave investigation of the dynamics of visual consciousness, expressed and lived through his very demanding paintings. The earliest works in this exhibition were, by some coincidence, my first exposure to Lang's odd and ferocious energy which seemed so extravagant and so at one with the hot yet coolly urbane, exultant yet desperate mood of Los Angeles in the transitional era of the late 1970s and early 1980s.

The work already had an uncanny syntax, moving and shifting from plane to plane, changing its pictorial language in some visually multicultural dance. Lang was then devoted to jagged, multicolored planes of painted and pasted color. He recycled elements of modernist abstraction while responding to the dizzying Los Angeles street show of torn and fragmented ads and messages with their undomesticated exotic hybrids of high and low culture. The work embodied and described a virtual nervous breakdown of a contemporary world at once familiar, terrifying, and strange. At the outset, Lang showed no interest in pleasant "arrangements" or even in fashionable "texts" but was driven to create a visual equivalent of late twentieth-century consciousness stalking the scary edges of urban life.

By the early 1980s, Lang already had a following among Los Angeles critics and collectors who were bold enough to handle the raucous, impolite energy his paintings and sculptures brought into otherwise elegantly cool collections of L.A. neopop and smartly conceptual art. His work was more accessible to those with a wide exposure to European art, to the visually shattered works of early twentieth-century Dadaists, like Schwitters and utopian Constructivists like Rodchenko, who cultivated provocative collisions of style and content.

Electric in their color, spilling over their edges with incident, introducing a disquieting and even troubling presence wherever they went, Lang's paintings and sculpture played a very public role in an optimistic moment in California postmodern culture which briefly challenged New York for artistic preeminence. He was part of a generation of young artists finally able to debunk old stereotypes of cultural regionalism as they roamed nomadically across the entire globe, a traveling tribe who worked alternately in Los Angeles and New York while remaining active in Europe, where the contemporary art environment was often more adventurous and rewarding.

Lang's education set the stage for his restlessly bicoastal life as he took off from his native Los Angeles in 1970 to enroll at the Whitney Studio Program in New York City. He returned to the West Coast in late 1971 to attend the California Institute of the Arts, Valencia, where he completed his B.A. in 1973 in the company of fellow students Ross Bleckner, Eric Fischl, and David Salle. Many of Lang's peers from Cal Arts pursued careers in New York immediately and with great success and critical acclaim. They were fueled by the conceptual approach to artistic practice taught by John Baldessari and others on the innovative and effective Cal Arts faculty.

In a characteristically introspective spirit, Lang opted to go to Yale University in 1973, where he finished an M.F.A. in 1975. It would be difficult to find a more vivid contrast of pedagogy and philosophy than these two programs, Cal Arts and Yale. Lang was aware of but determined to avoid entanglement in the elegant and systematic theories of color in painting introduced by Josef Albers during the 1950s and carried on through several subsequent generations of Yale faculty and students. He was also unconvinced by the linguistically and sociologically driven theoretical issues then featured throughout Yale's humanities curriculum, ideas that soon found adherents in many universities in America.

A Fulbright Grant allowed Lang to spend more than a year in Spain where he preferred Barcelona with its familiar sunny climate, wonderful yet highly focused museums, and the wildly colorful architecture of Antonio Gaudí. There is scant evidence of the formal and elegant character of historical Spain in Lang's 1975 *Barcelona Painting* [Figure 1], featuring a smiling Mickey Mouse surveying a mountainous landscape while other compartments of this jarring, ungraceful, thickly-painted work speak volumes about Lang's delight in her beaches, marinas, and warm sun. Living in the present moment, unrepentantly independent of art-historical heroes, rejecting clever ironies, Lang had already begun to find his starting point as an artist.

Returning to Los Angeles, Lang carried with him both a new sophistication and a greater willingness to look and listen to the L.A. urban environment, which spoke in many dialects and reflected a wide range of moods. Living in a loft in a downtown industrial warehouse, Lang created an odd paradise filled with tropical plants, exotic birds, a favorite dog, postcards and letters providing reminiscences of his time in Europe. It was a gentle place with a warmth and easy graciousness not often seen or cultivated in artists' working environments.

It was in this very personal domain just an arm's length from the chaos of the streets that Gary Lang created a still troubling but deeply memorable group of painted sculptures he called "weapons" [Figures 2a and 2b]. Handmade, featuring metal spikes or multiple wooden teeth, sometimes formed in the image of bullets [Figure 5b] or simple old-fashioned bomb casings, they expressed almost perfectly the tension, genuine physical danger, and undeniable creativity of Los Angeles in the early 1980s. It was well known that local gangs often created crude weapons and used them on each other—and occasionally on unrelated passers-by.

Few people frequenting the polite and fashionable gallery scene then flourishing among the young boomer generation of Los Angeles had ever contemplated owning, or even touching, such objects. Lang's weapons had an appealing sensuality, a high degree of tactility, and innovative colors and patterns. Some were so large that they dominated an entire gallery with their kaleidoscopic imagery and invasive physicality. Wild patterns suggesting moments of spiritual and physical intoxication covered some of Lang's sculpture and many of his paintings. Many viewers found them provocative but disturbing. One remembers hearing whispered comments, uncomfortable laughter, personal experiences of urban violence recounted with false bravado, and almost universal speculation about the intent of the artist.

How could one put together the serious, good-humored personality of this artist with his aggressive painted sculpture that alternatively seduced and troubled his audience? In retrospect, Lang's "weapons" of the 1980s seem touchingly homemade and evocative of a time merely predicting the eventual course of human events in the most elemental way. In truth, Lang was perhaps more concerned and consumed than many in his artistic audience by the life he witnessed daily on the streets of L.A. Longing for harmony and a state of general and personal well-being, he tried to achieve repose in the neo-pastoral environment of his studio. In his "weapons," Lang elevated and abstracted a crude sculptural medium of human exchange. Talismanic and still powerful, they have a vividness and theatricality that would linger productively in his painting.

Gary Lang both sensed the short-lived nature of the urban artistic renaissance going on in L.A. and knew that his own evolution required him to move to New York City, which he did in 1985. Paintings such as *Isn't It Wonderful* [Figure 4] show how secretly fond he was of the then old-fashioned language of modernist abstraction. It is redolent of the distinctly American palette of Morgan Russell, Stuart Davis, or Patrick Henry Bruce. Jazzy shifts from strict flat triangles of primary color to almost descriptive passages of grass green evidence a seriously playful spirit that has characterized Lang's work from the outset. Perhaps no one enjoys breaking rules more than a person who has effectively internalized them.

The wild complexity of Lang's delirious syntax finds its apotheosis in *Night Life* [Figure 8], a major painting of 1987. In it, Lang provides a vast panoramic tour through New York's extravagant zones of entertainment, pleasure, and excess which were spinning down toward entropy in that memorable year of the stock market debacle. Because he was working part-time in a prominent nightclub, Lang had a front row seat at Manhattan's club scene, which he saw as increasingly threadbare and decadent. In *Night Life*, a row of fists laid cross-wise at the work's center, point pistols directly at the viewer. A riot of pattern makes the work spin off at odd angles and segments it into distinctly colored and configured zones. At its heart, *Night Life*, spins around a rainbow-hued hexagon so tenderly realized that it seems to announce a spiritual renewal in the midst of emotional chaos and the array of sensuous temptations and perils laid before the viewer.

Aspects of each element of his life experience, background, and education have lodged in the complex art of Gary Lang. His knowing command of painting's many visual languages and physical possibilities, allows him to stimulate the viewer's immanent awareness of our visual world. His work brings together a remarkable array of issues of critical importance if certain dimensions of the art of painting are to survive into the next century. While many of his generation located their painting careers within the domain of narrative—calculating that the subjects of history, politics, cultural identity, or sociology were vastly more interesting than the epistemological issues lying within the domain and language of painting itself—Lang remained quietly, intently focused upon the daily miracles occurring in his studio. Abstract painting took on a more overtly conceptual tone, as his contemporaries quoted modern masters with a cold and vehement irony. Lang watched his contemporaries tearing apart the spiritual tradition of abstract painting but seemed to know that they would not succeed.

In much of the painting of the 1980s, personal and authentic emotion was removed from the arena of art and replaced by synthetic expressions derived from media sources and delivered in the voice of ironic quotation. To attempt a frank, personal statement in one's art was to risk ridicule and forfeit a chance to participate in that self-assured, self-congratulatory art scene. At the time, Lang seemed extraordinarily out of step for one so connected and aware of the tides of critical fashion. His work, for all its bad-boy theatricality and dizzying syntax, is quite simply a search for the spiritual through visual experience. Choosing his words haltingly and carefully, struggling to describe what he feels and sees and knows within the process of realizing his work, his conversation often sounds like a plainer reiteration of Kandinsky speaking in the 1910s or some of Mondrian's flights of speculation grounded within the realm of art. When he is questioned closely, it becomes apparent that he has not recently reread their essays, even if he probably encountered them sometime in his education.

The odd and marvelous experiences with light, space, contradiction, and paradox he describes arise in the everyday routine of his studio. Slowly the state of fragmentation that so characterized his early work gave way to a satisfying wholeness. His kaleidoscopic color remained, but it acquired a new disciplined coherence as each element was allowed to reveal itself slowly and quietly while contributing to the work in its entirety. He had not adopted anyone's formula but had painstakingly arrived at a condition of mastery expressive of his own inner nature. Recklessness transformed itself into mature, unwavering assertion.

Watching Gary Lang's habits and evolution as a painter, it has been interesting to see a recurring scenario unfold as he goes through important changes in his work. He begins with a group of small paintings, some only six or seven inches in either dimension, and devotes himself to a cycle of many small works. One often has the impression that they will constitute his final goal. Over the years, however, it has become clear that this stage is only the opening act of a long drama which is likely to reach its climax on a grand scale once the imagery is able to speak with an authentic voice. A small untitled painting of 1987—featuring a group of ascending concentric circles hovering over a brightly colored field of bright horizontal lines—is such a beginning.

My own introduction to this work occurred in 1988 when Gary Lang appeared one day, carrying a small circular painting under his arm and wearing an uncharacteristically serene expression. The little painting pulsated in space and was full of lively push and pull. Muted circles of olive and earth-gray alternated with circular bands of electric blue and warm rose. At closer inspection, the colors seemed individually unremarkable. Their combinations and the format itself created this vital presence. Full of confidence and looking forward to the playing out of this artistic intuition, Lang was poised for a new wave of work.

It is not surprising that Lang's critical fortunes improved dramatically after 1988. Many solo exhibitions in New York featured the dramatic circle paintings, and critics speculated upon their possible meanings, virtually always discovering their metaphysical core. Several writers brought up Lang's provocative color and characterized it as a challenge to usual norms of beauty in painting.

Lang has always included a few flamboyant colors in his palette: irradiated pink, spring green, lipstick red. These are memorable but impolite colors one often associates with debased consumer goods of the 1950s and with psychedelic fashions and art of the late 1960s. Children also favor extravagant color, but most mature artists tend to drop such hues from consideration. These are, however, the very colors that animate Lang's circle paintings of the 1990s, giving them a glowing presence supported by a subordinate range of dark blues, browns, and warm blacks.

Another factor supporting the success of this body of work is the beautiful technique Lang evolved in the application of his color to canvas. The central core of each work was painted several times in thin glazes. Initially, he followed the circular contours of the form. Once established, this understructure provides a base for new strata of radiating strokes moving outward from the center. These suggested some inner source of brightly colored light. Flat tints alternate and interrupt translucent ones in an irregular rhythm, making it impossible to consider the whole as a mere repetitious pattern of predictable relationships. Surprise and revelation occur again and again as the viewer moves from part to whole and eventually follows the urge to plunge back into the spinning, glowing core. Lang's raw, dazzling colors regain the rapturous beauty and fascination they have in a child's naive eye, allowing us to see them without prejudice once again.

On several occasions Gary Lang fulfilled his desire to create a circle painting on a grand scale. An early painting created on a large wall of the Mark Quint Gallery in San Diego in 1990 was carried out virtually in the spirit of an Indian sand painting. It was beautifully and painstakingly crafted with all the complexity and care of a work on canvas. At the end of the exhibition, the painting vanished under a new coat of gallery paint and survives only in photographic documentation and memory. This was also the season of a happy new relationship with the painter Ruth Pastine who married Lang in 1993. She assisted in the crafting of Lang's Quint Gallery installation, and her support and understanding of the purposes and processes of painting have continued to be a source of strength in the lives of both artists.

Lang's painted installations reveal a number of important things about his work and his current state of mind. While creating them, he seems to dwell within a charmed and focused state of being. It is clear that he is utterly secure in the knowledge of what he is going to do. Intellectually and technically, he has resolved the central questions about the image and its expressive intent. This leaves him free to explore just how the work is to unfold. As each color is laid down, it proposes its own array of possible responses from the painter. Lang is always stalking the edge of disaster, hungry for surprise and eager to do something so odd and arbitrary that it just might not work at all. He will often sequester a particularly dominant hue in one edge or corner of a painting while daring the rest of the work to come to terms with it. He will build up a complex area of a painting to a degree unmatched anywhere else in the work, only to counterbalance it with an equally compelling but different set of elements and keep it all in splendid and continuous motion. Upsetting, amusing and deeply interesting, these are masterworks of painterly syntax.

These tendencies and habits are played out most rigorously in another body of work begun in the late 1980s and continuing into the present decade. They are the horizontally and vertically oriented grid compositions or "plaid paintings," as the artist has irreverently termed them [Figures 12 and 14]. Linearity is the ruling principle in these dizzying, hard-hitting encounters with speed and color. They exist in marked contrast to the meditative quietude of the circular canvases of the same time period. Full of the frenetic energy of urban life, Lang's plaid paintings recall the unceasing interrelatedness of Piet Mondrian's final works created in New York City from late 1940 to early 1944, his experiments with interwoven colored tapes to create an animated grid, and his famous homage to New York, the *Broadway Boogie-Woogie* of 1944.

Lang's plaid paintings have just as much in common with the performed character of action painting—which quickly becomes apparent upon closer inspection. He invites the viewer to follow each colored line on its transit across the surface, a journey involving multiple points of intersection and layering as one color moves over or under another. Bold, thick linear elements stand as architectonic pillars screening the interior zones of the painting. Quick, slender members traverse the lateral course of the implied grid with graceful speed. Nothing is static, everything moves, undulating in space like the smoothly unsteady horizon line of a compass at sea. Color plays a major role, but it is impossible to characterize these paintings by a dominant hue. Rather, each work seems to have an almost musical tonality arising out of the combined assertions of several strong coloristic voices. Examining them closely, one can often sense the season of the year in which they were painted or the emotional tenor of the artist's world as they evolved.

Out of this highly personal syntax came a sublime group of paintings so finely wrought and optically complex that Lang called them his "mirror paintings" [Figures 16 and 20]. In them, all deep space disappears and is replaced by a shimmer of infinitely graded colored light caused by a delicate network of interlaced colored lines. They seem to throw their light back toward the viewer and to dazzle—indeed mesmerize—until the very nature of this color is difficult to describe. Certainly the number of hues and their graded proximity brings retinal saturation into play. One becomes more aware of the sheer presence of light than of any specific color. Lang's approach is so plainly intuitive that the work has a remarkable vulnerability and a good deal of emotional impact. Each of these paintings appears as a revelation, a gift that can never be reconstructed or repeated. Their compelling quietude and beauty recall the meditative nature of Lang's mature circle paintings, also the end of an important concept in its development.

Throughout Lang's career, his pursuit of a meaningful image has been accompanied by a need for an appropriate and often innovative format, for example, the three-dimensional painted weapons, the small and also very large circular canvases, the site works and murals, and the grandly scaled gridded paintings of recent years. There is a strong element of theatricality in Lang's choice of format, just as there is an assertive emotional element to his color. Putting such dynamic and potentially disturbing elements into play, Lang risks calling attention to one aspect of a work to the detriment of the whole. He seems to enjoy, indeed crave, this sense of danger and drama. Through time he has gained an astonishing mastery of these treacherous tools. He can now achieve a state of calm resonance out of colors seldom seen outside a child's crayon box. Scale now supports his ability to speak to the audience and his eagerness to offer something memorable and important. Color, scale, and process are now so firmly a part of his æsthetic that their disruptive power is set free.

Gary Lang is a valuable and important American painter within his talented and celebrated generation. He has taken hold of the complex mechanisms of advanced modernist painting and used them with affection, integrity, and a sense of high adventure. True to his time, Lang almost obscures the tenderness and lyricism of his enterprise behind a brash facade of sassy color and quick pictorial moves. His work demands attention and does not let the viewer out of its grasp without a struggle. The pleasures of this work are deep and genuine but they are not easy. It is clear that Lang has known for quite a while that the world is not an easy place.

But through his art, the disquietude, the noise, the rumble of urban life, the disillusionment of our time are held at arm's length; and a glimpse of something transcendent emerges from the fray. For Gary Lang it can be no other way. To merely offer the outcome of his adventure would be to deny its authenticity and relevance to daily life. Each work requires that we join him on his artistic journey, experiencing our own revelations and outcomes each step of the way.

I *Barcelona Painting,* 1975
   acrylic on canvas
   40 × 13 inches

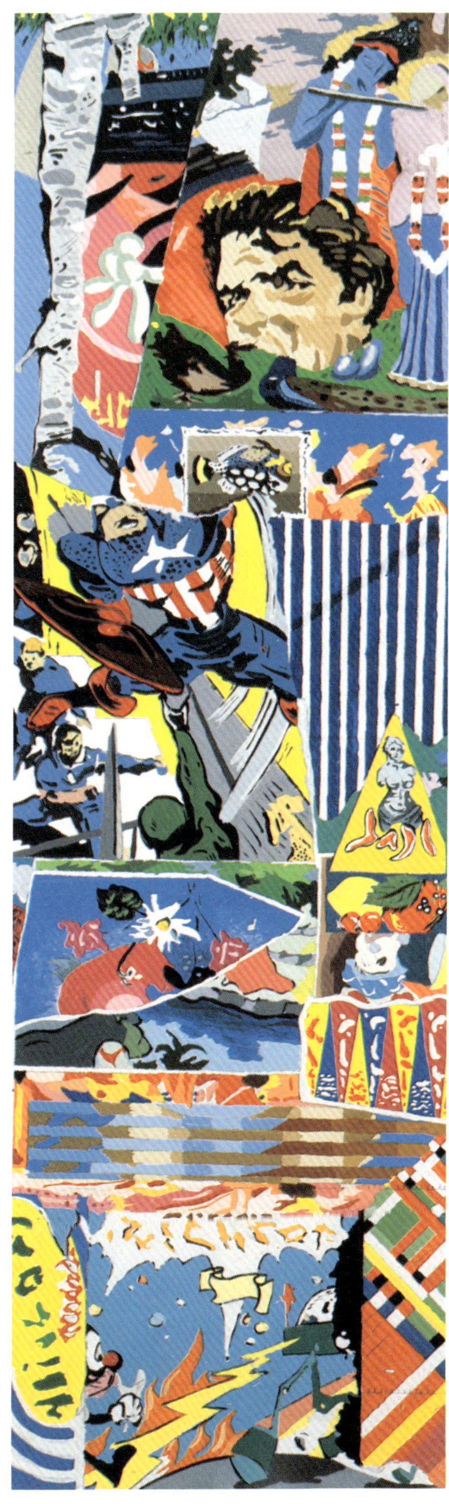

2a *Weapon*, 1980
    enamel, monofilament, and aluminum
    11 × 4 × 4 inches

2b *Weapon*, 1980
    aluminum and rubber
    13 × 4 × 4 inches

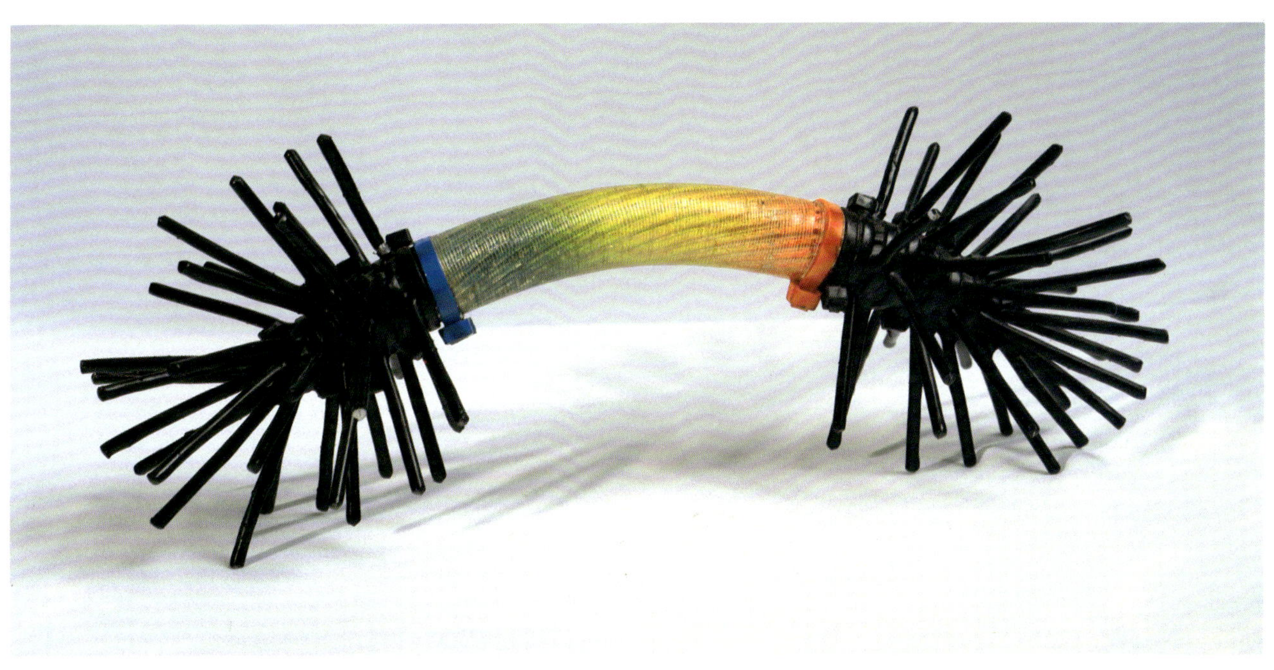

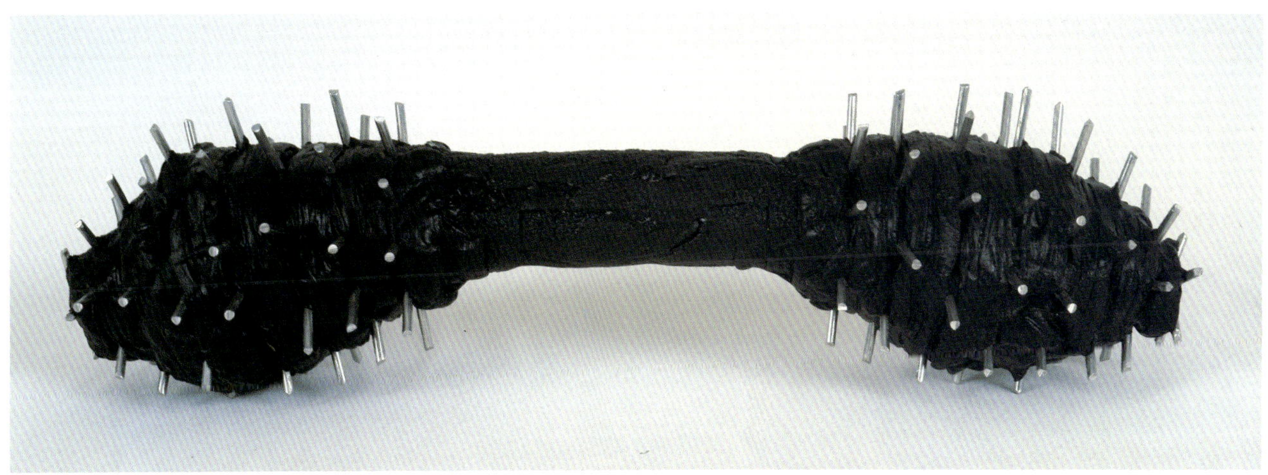

3 *Dried in Sound,* 1981
   oil and acrylic on canvas
   84 × 58 inches

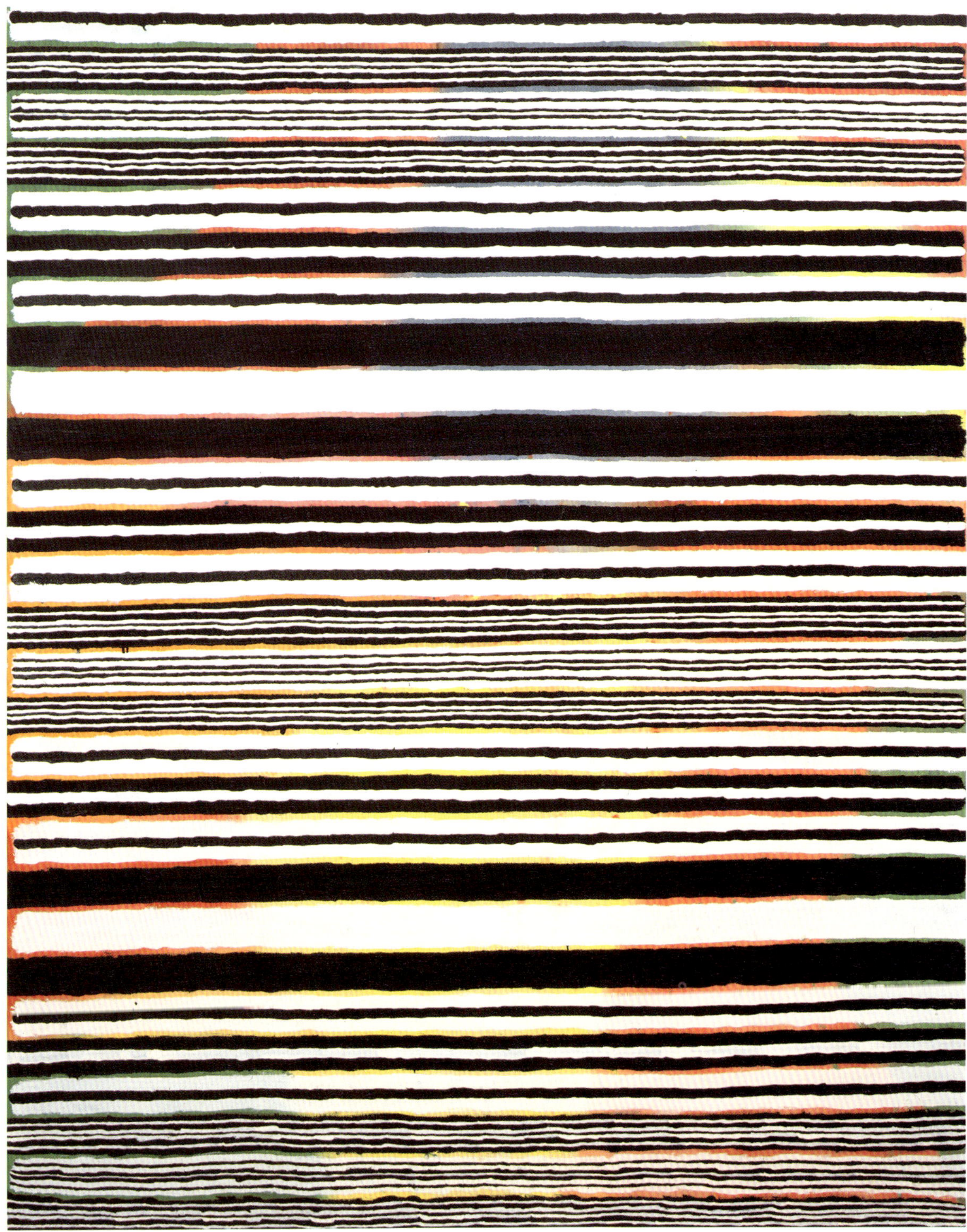

4 *Isn't It Wonderful*, 1981
   oil and acrylic on canvas
   17 × 9¾ inches

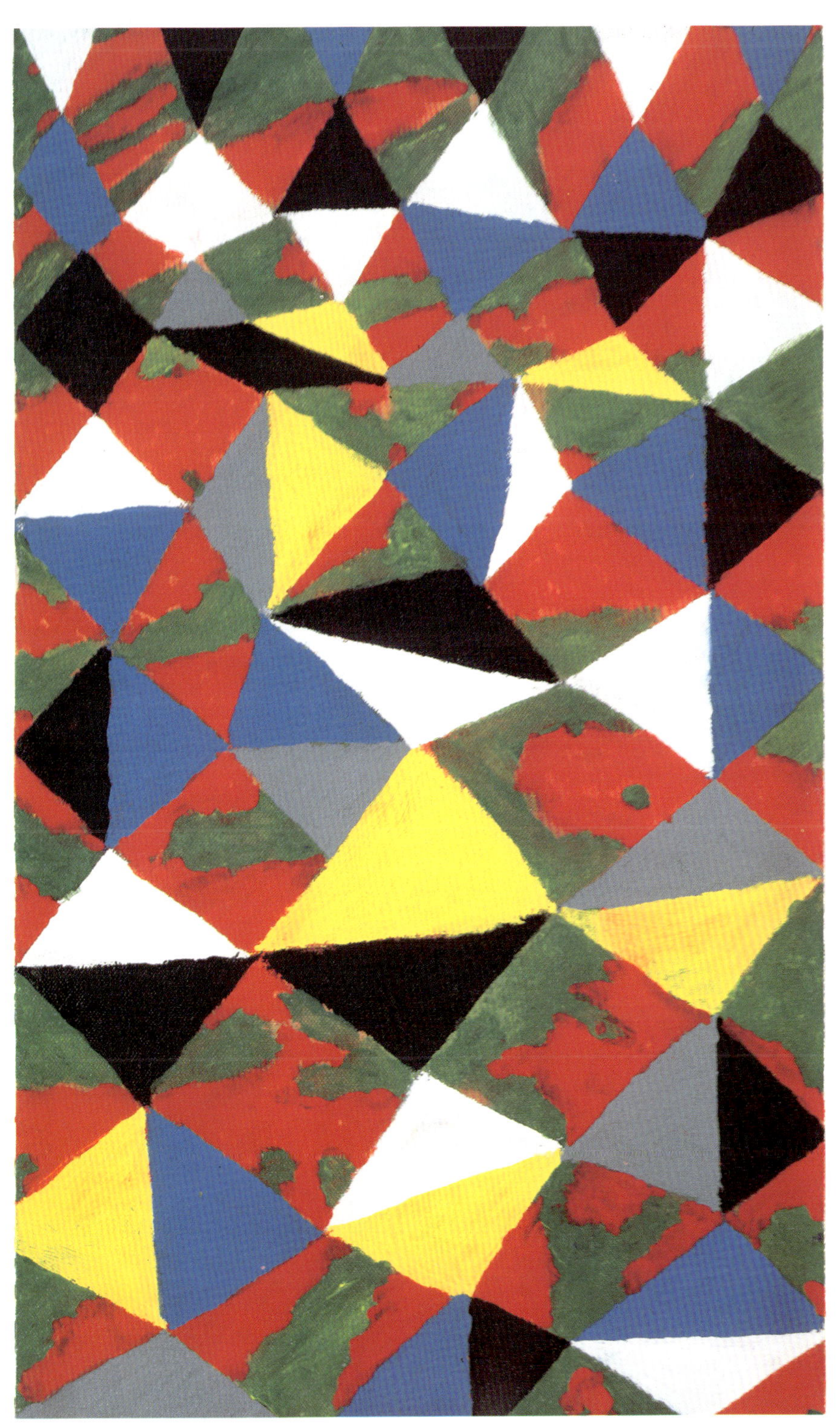

5a *Urn,* 1982
    acrylic, tape and wood
    29 × 18 × 18 inches

5b *Bullet,* 1982
    lacquer on wood
    17 × 5¼ × 5¼ inches

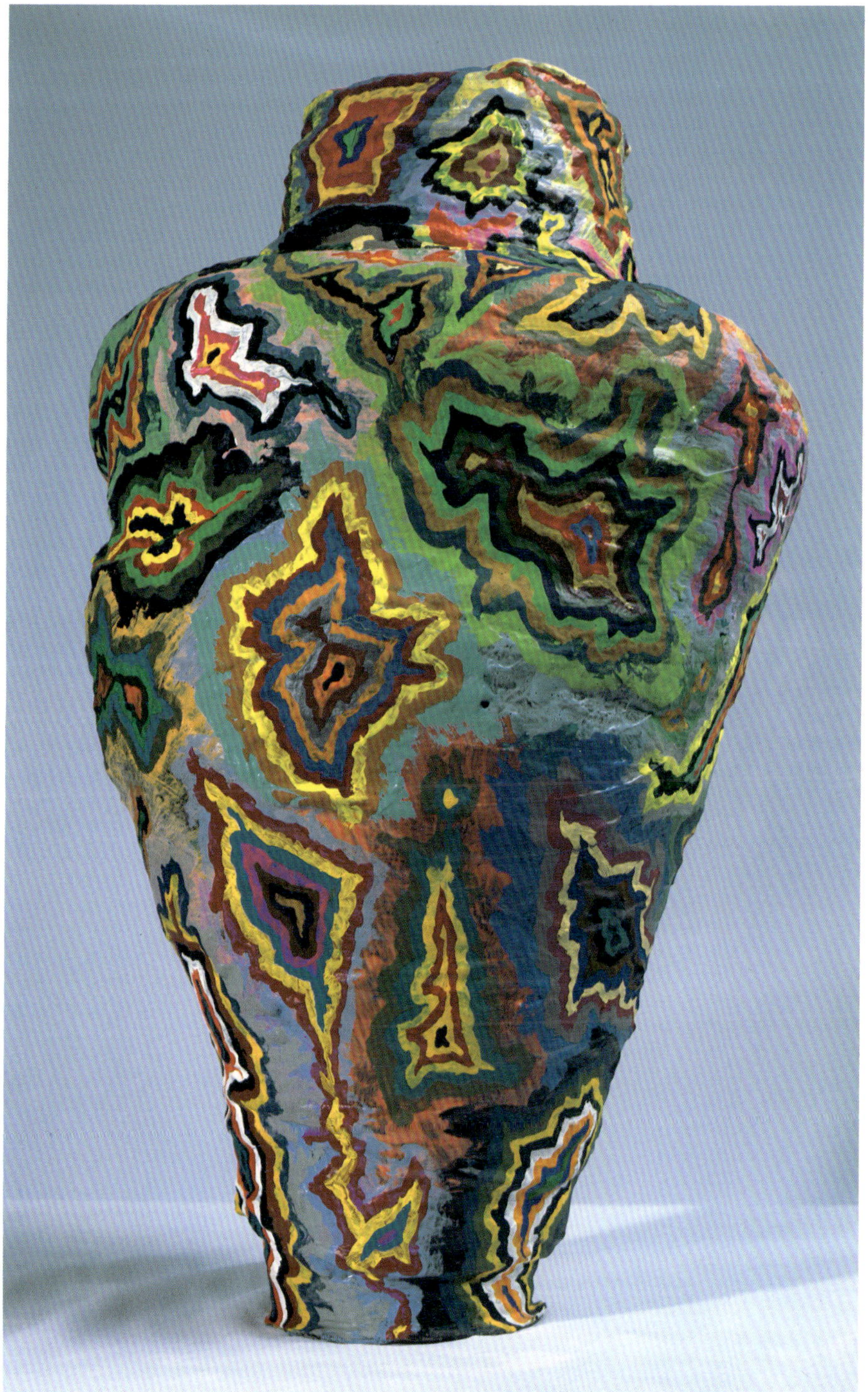

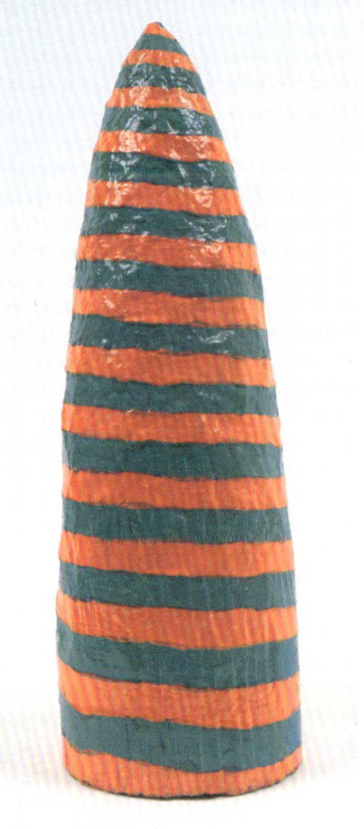

6 *The Loss Promotes the Gain*, 1983
   paper and staples (aggraphage)
   size and elements variable, detail

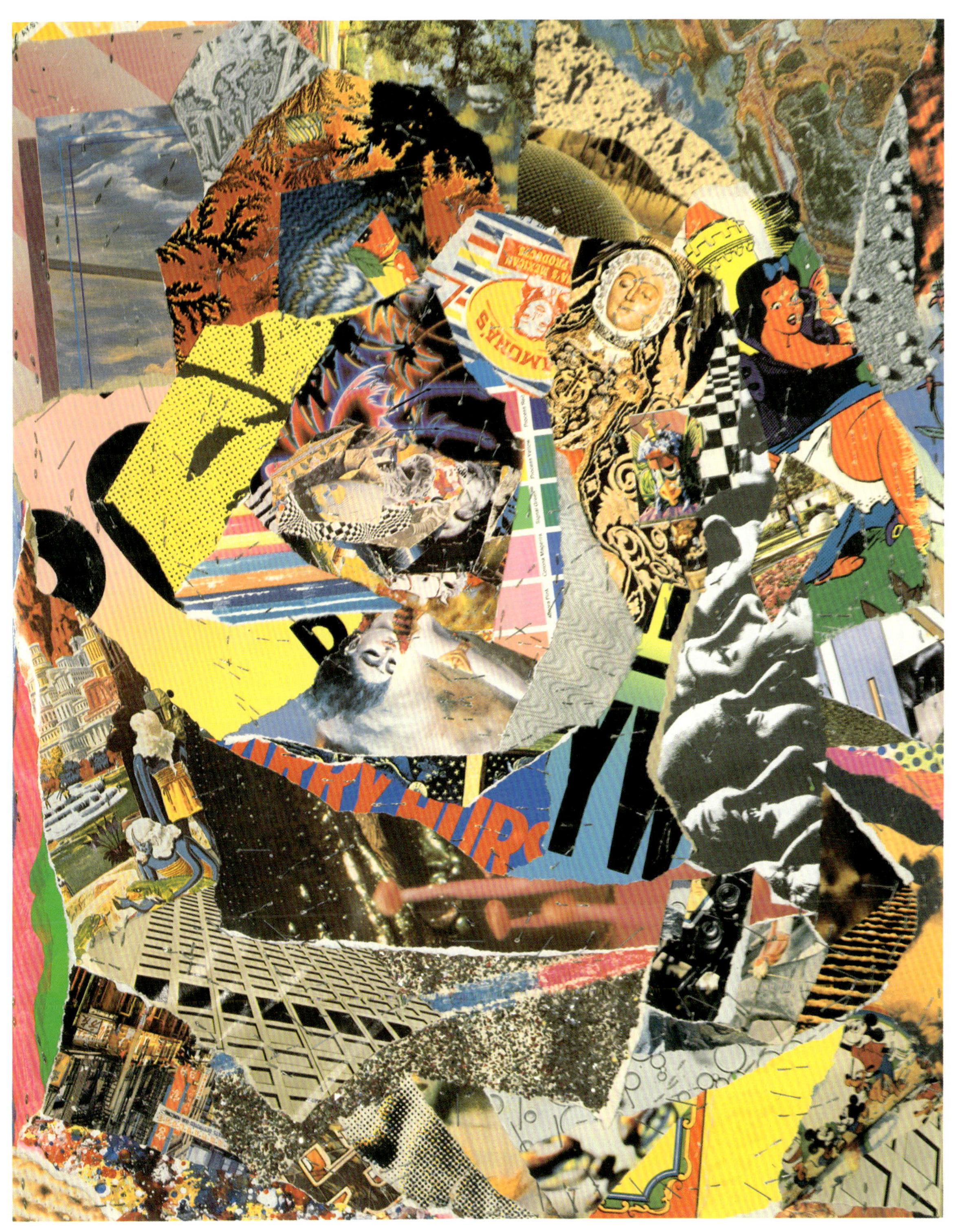

7 *Barefoot in the Studio—Better Than Milk,* 1985–86
oil and acrylic on canvas
84 × 60 inches

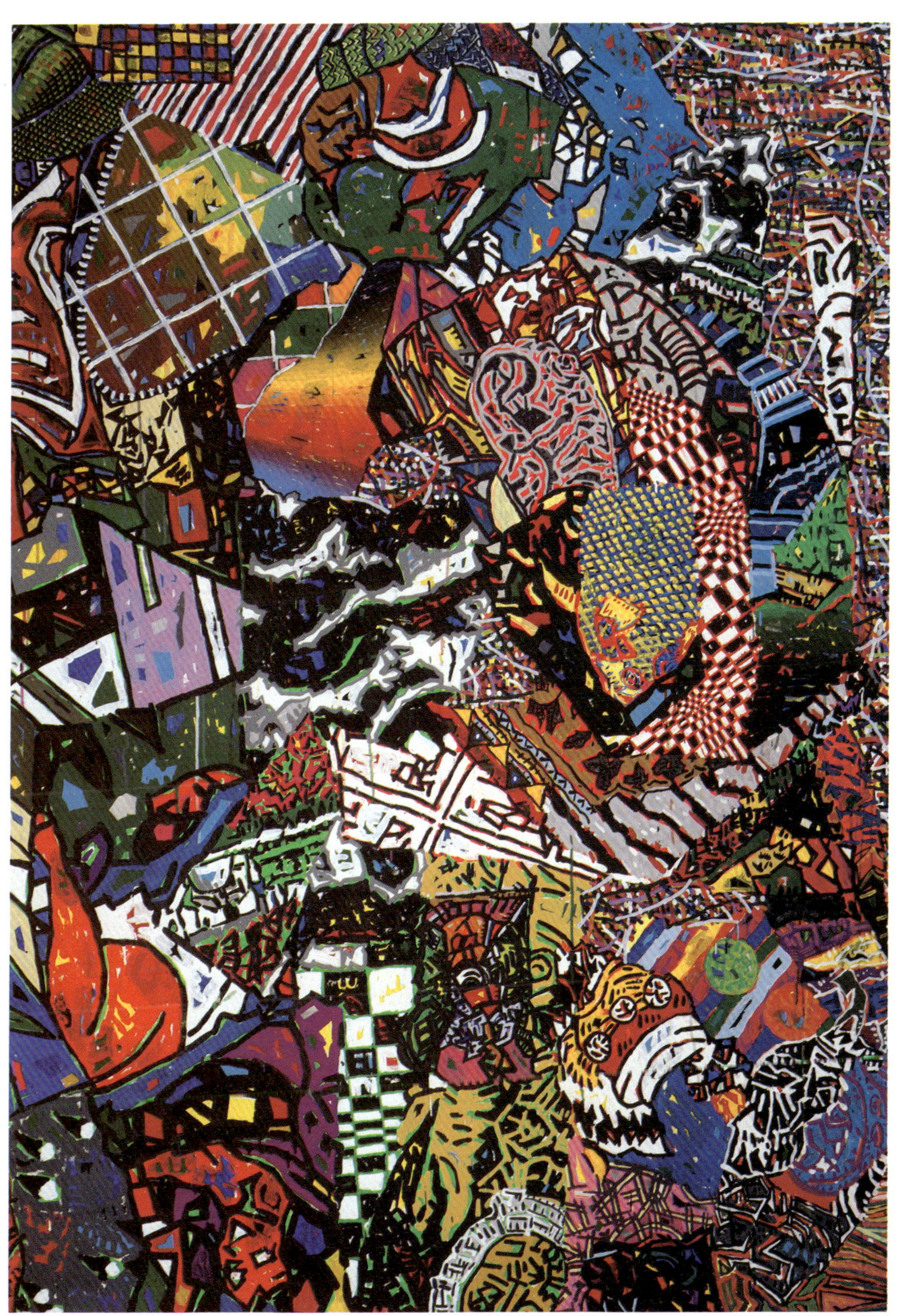

8 *Night Life*, 1987
acrylic on canvas
96 × 72 inches

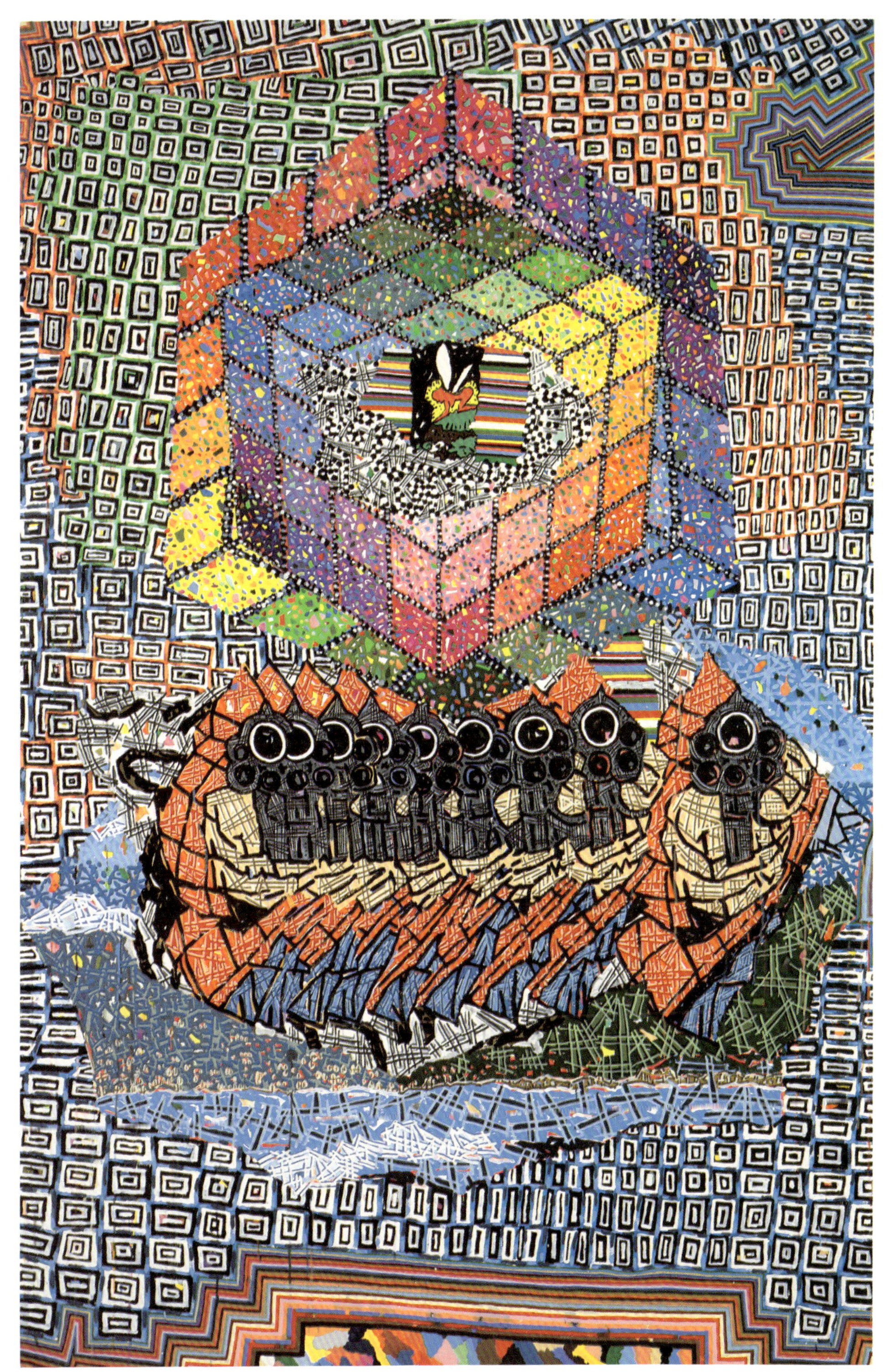

9 *Foo Lion,* 1987
   acrylic and wood
   44 × 32 × 30 inches

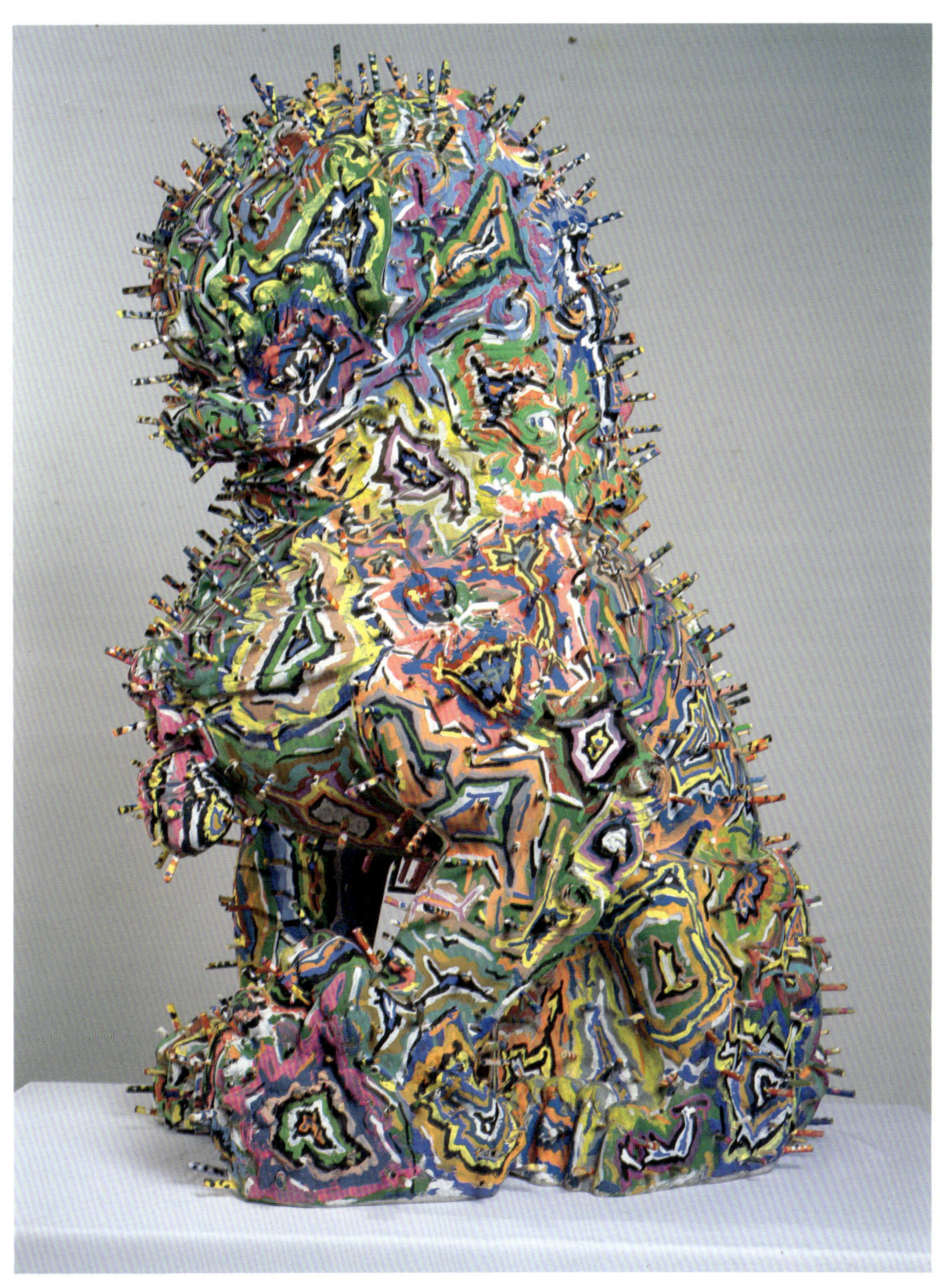

10 *Maverick*, 1988
    acrylic on canvas
    156 × 96 inches

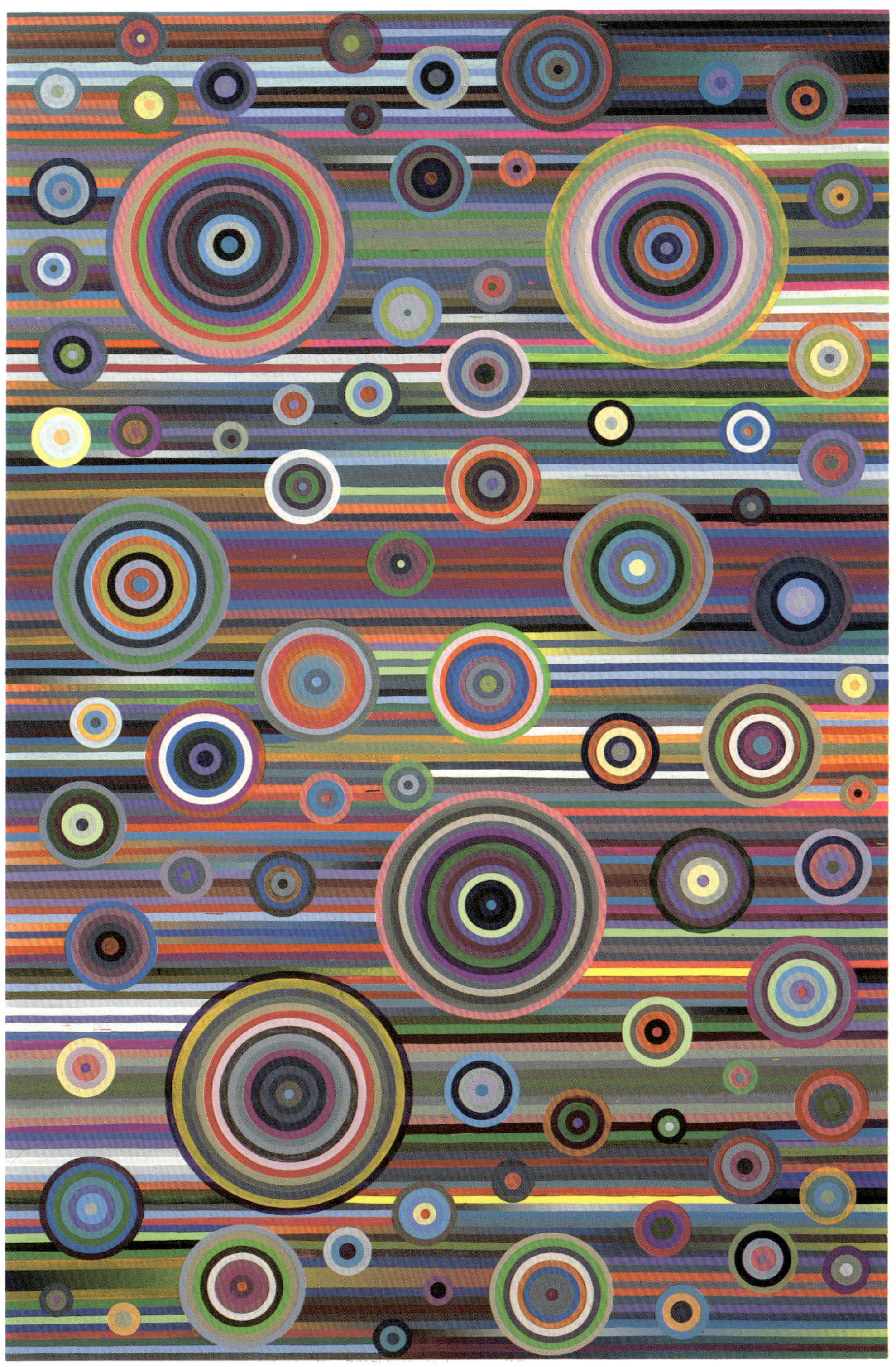

11 *Fez*, 1988–89
    acrylic on canvas
    43 × 43 inches

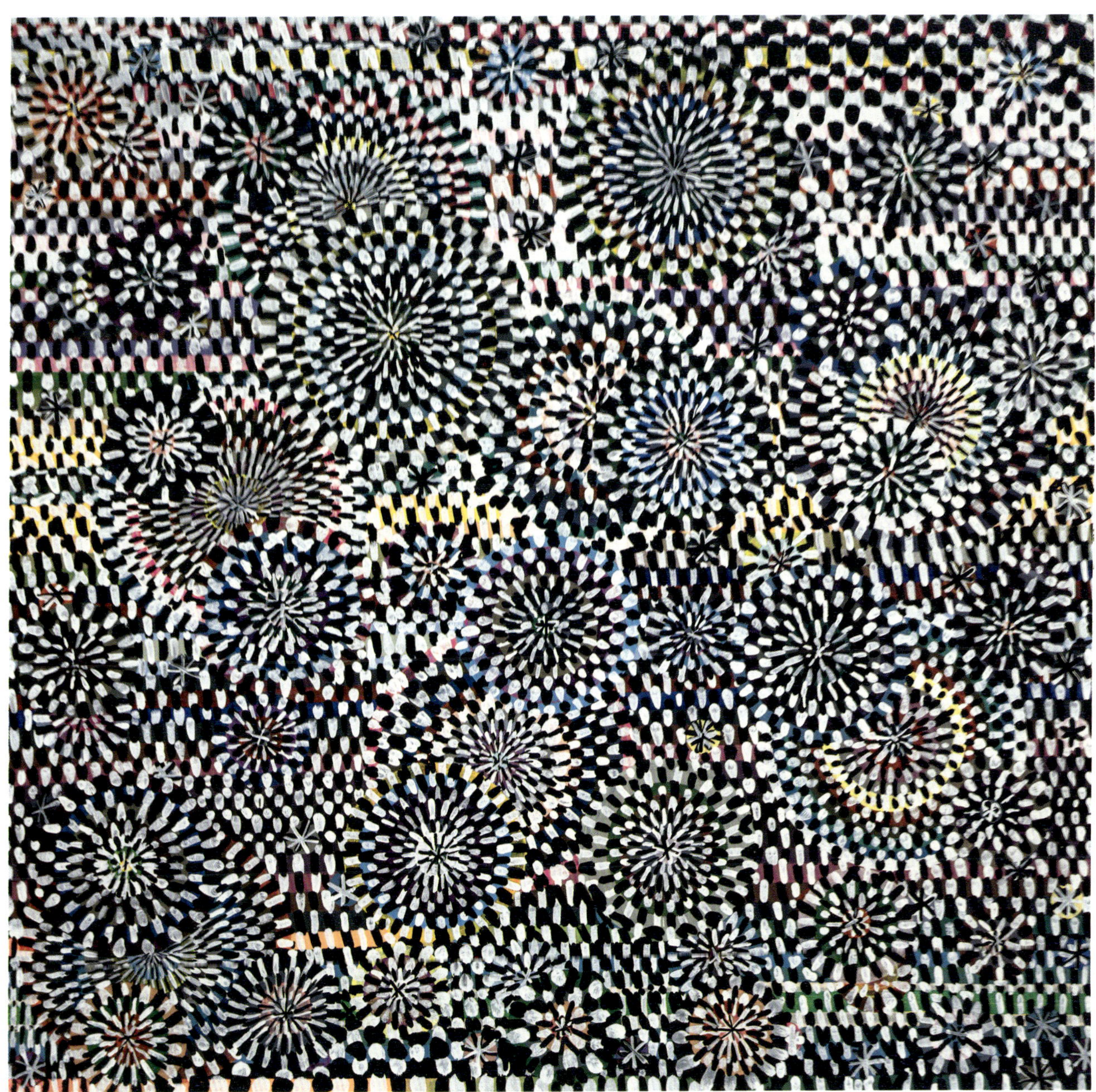

12 *Plaid Painting,* 1989
acrylic on canvas
84 × 84 inches

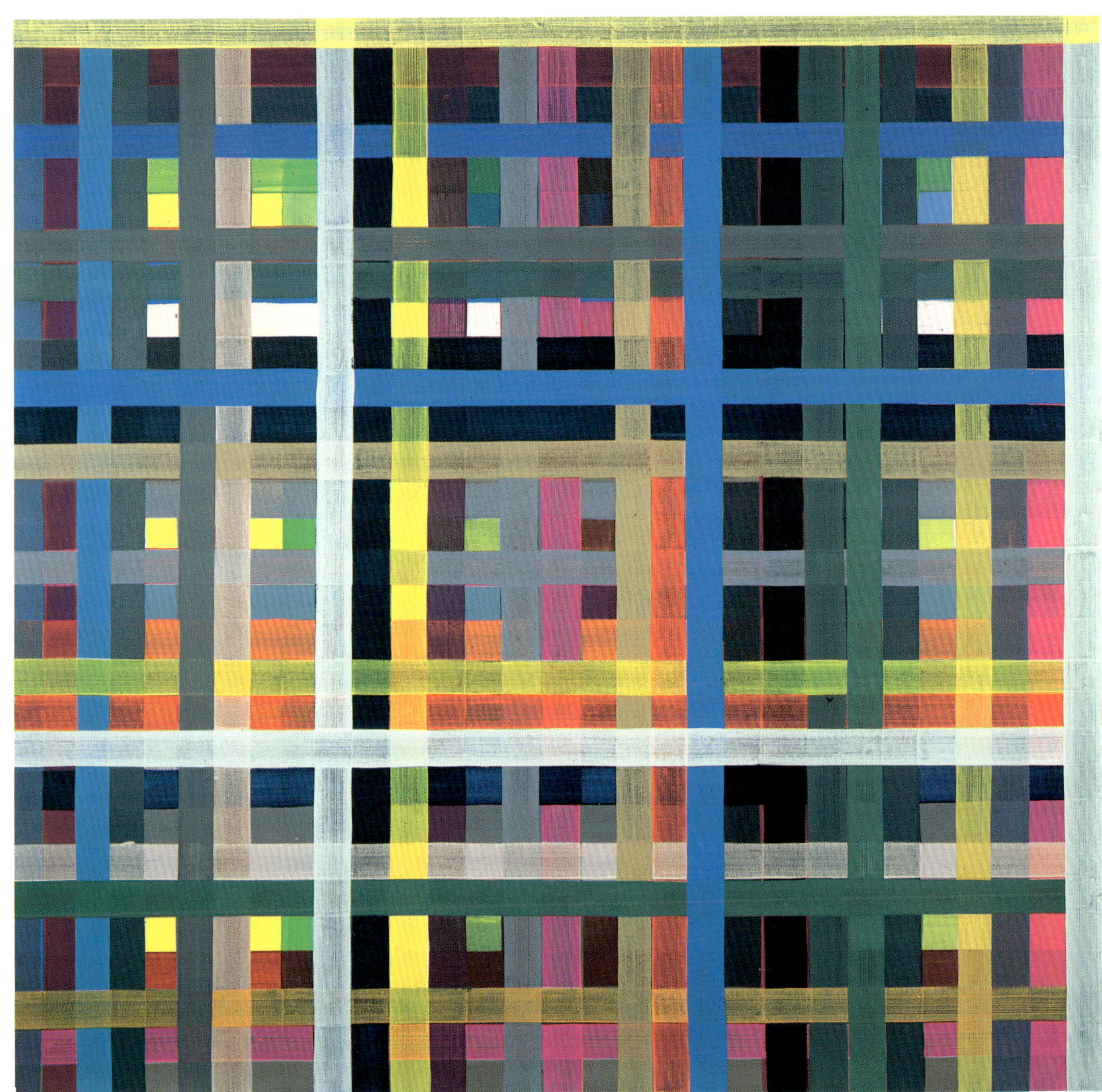

13 *Full Circle*, 1990
   acrylic on canvas
   84 inches diameter

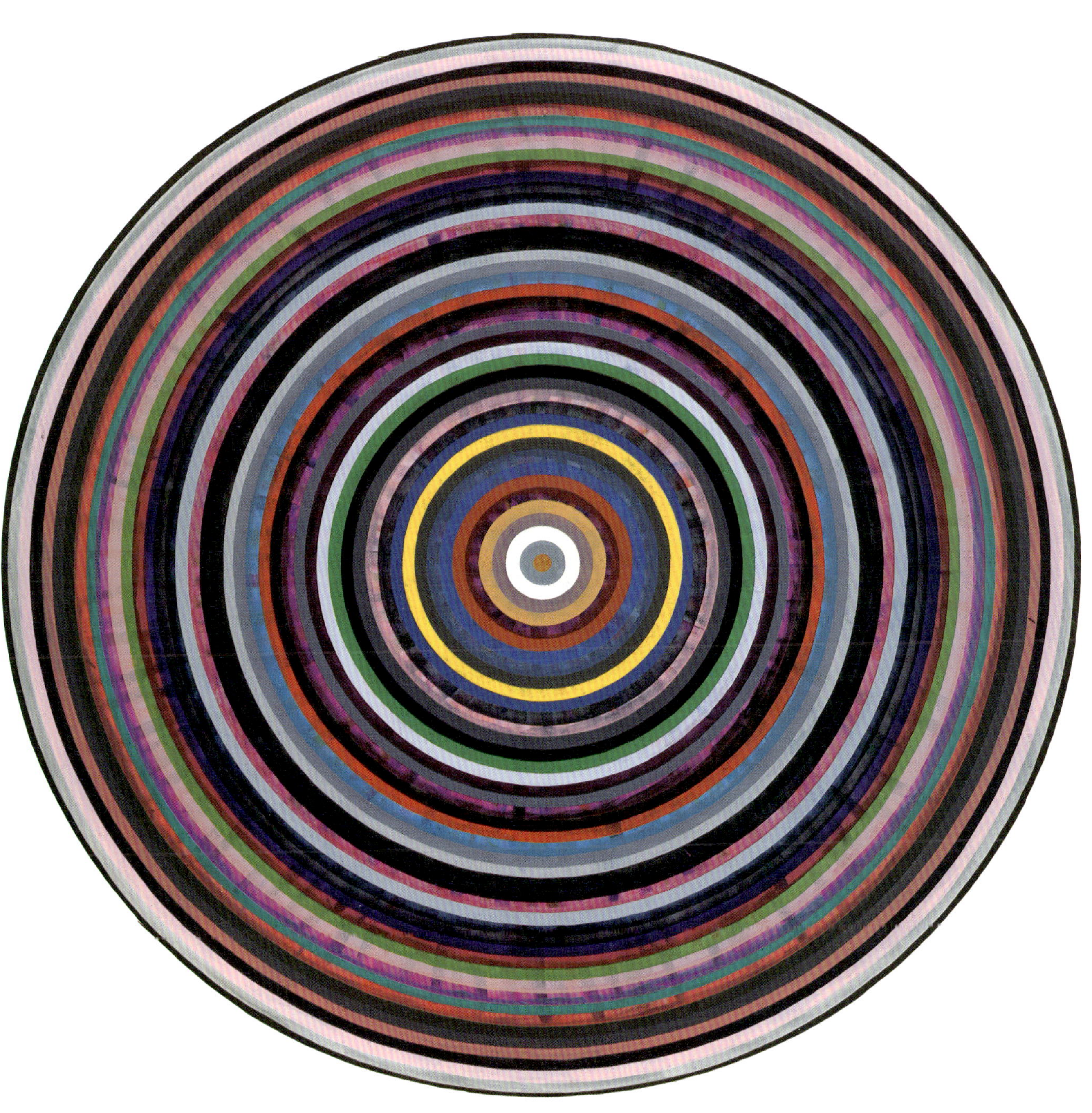

14 *Night Light,* 1990
    acrylic on canvas
    72 × 60 inches

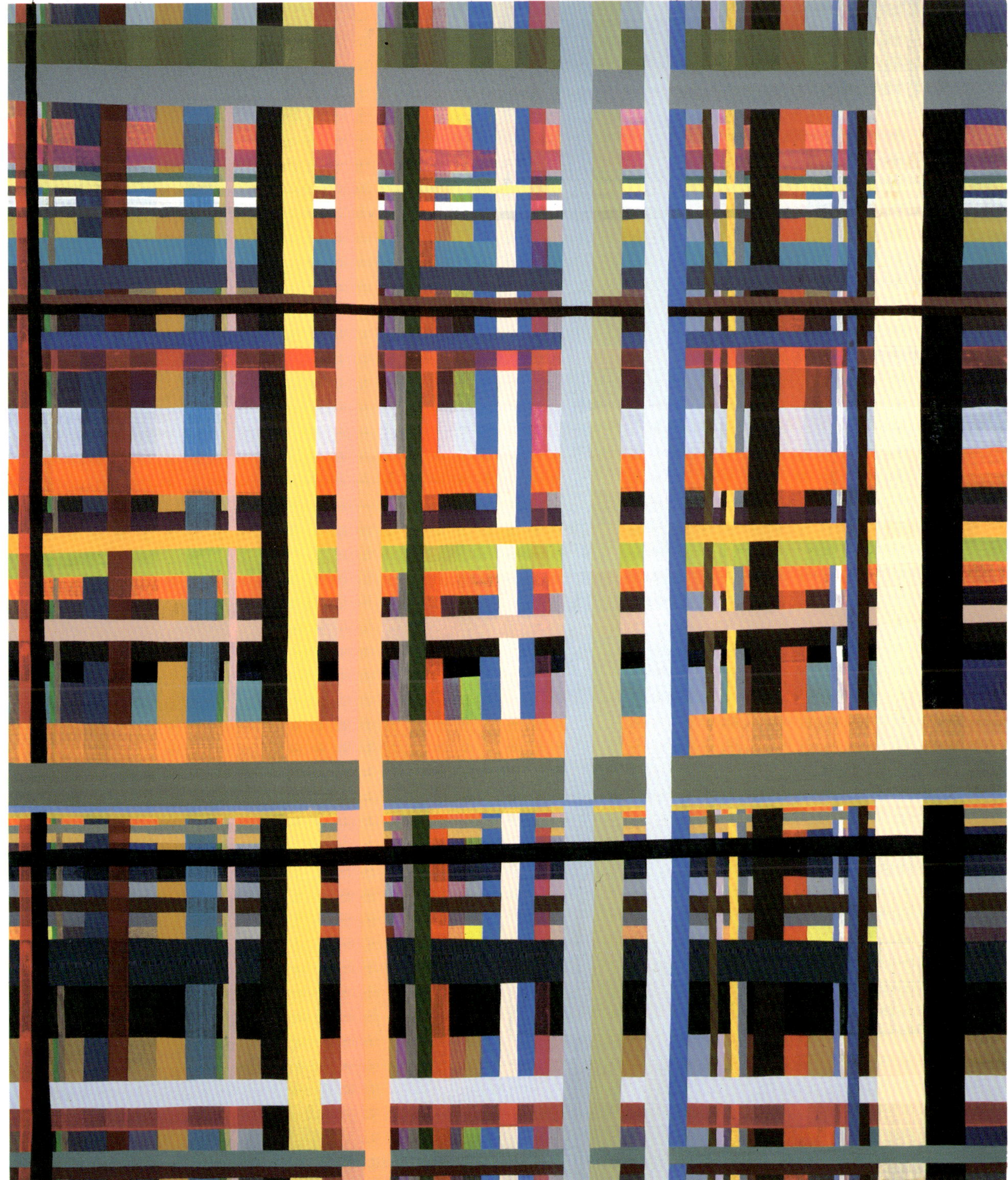

15 *Prayers,* 1991
    acrylic on canvas
    60 inches diameter

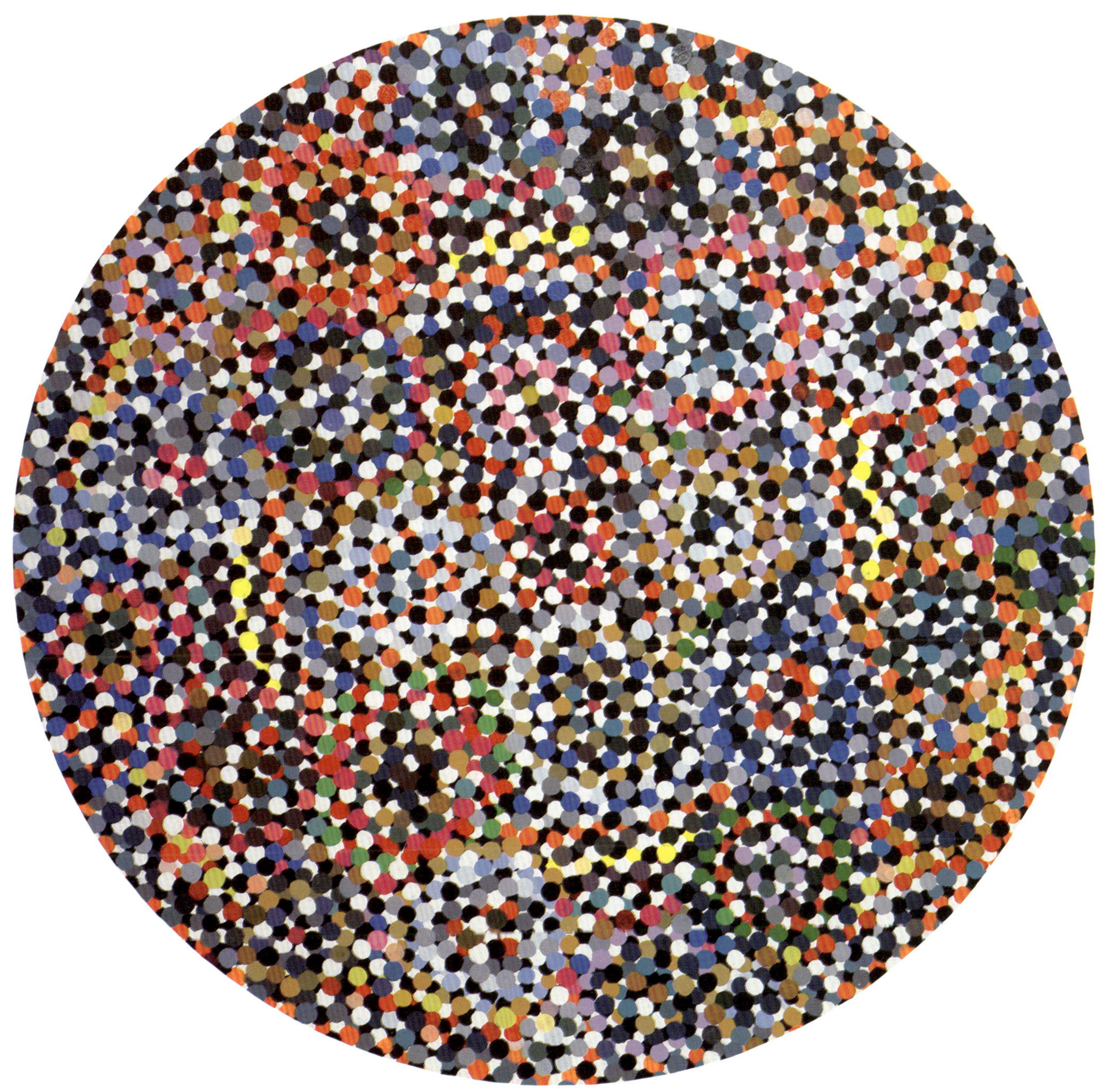

16 *Waving*, 1992
    acrylic on canvas
    113 × 113 inches

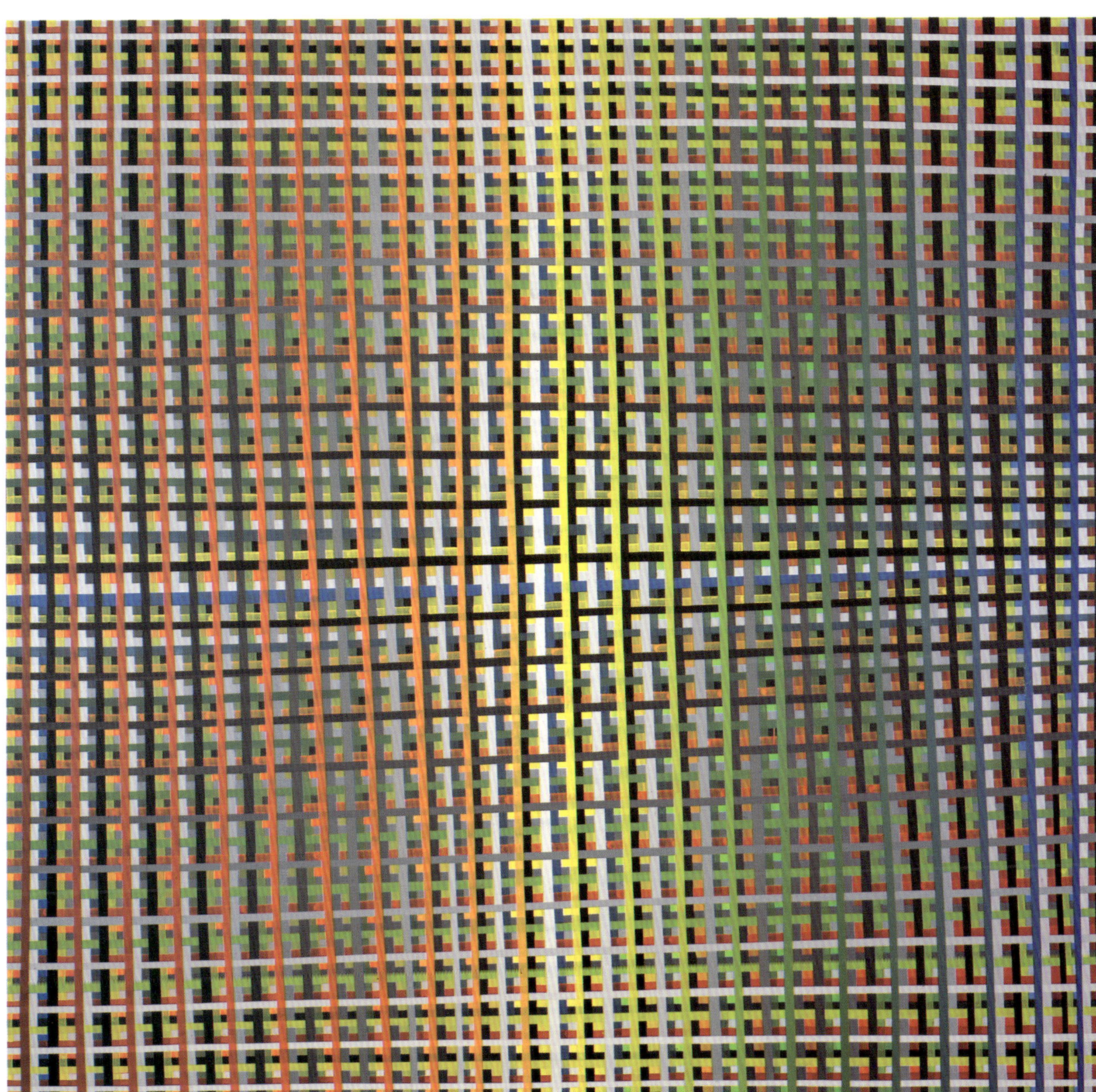

17 *Ruth's Truths,* 1993
acrylic on canvas
60 × 60 inches

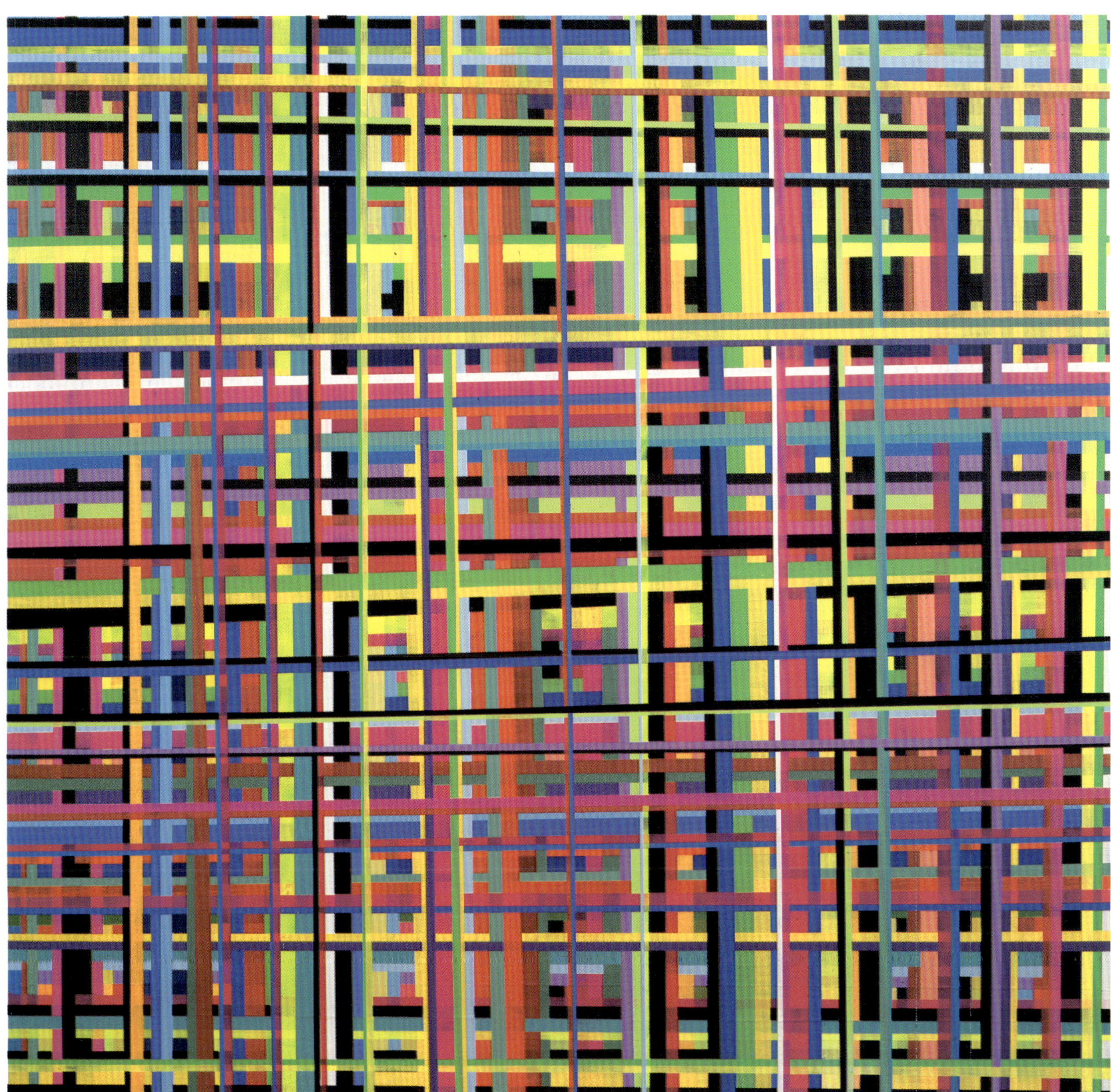

18 *Processing Funk and Wonder #2*, 1994
acrylic on canvas
63 × 63 inches

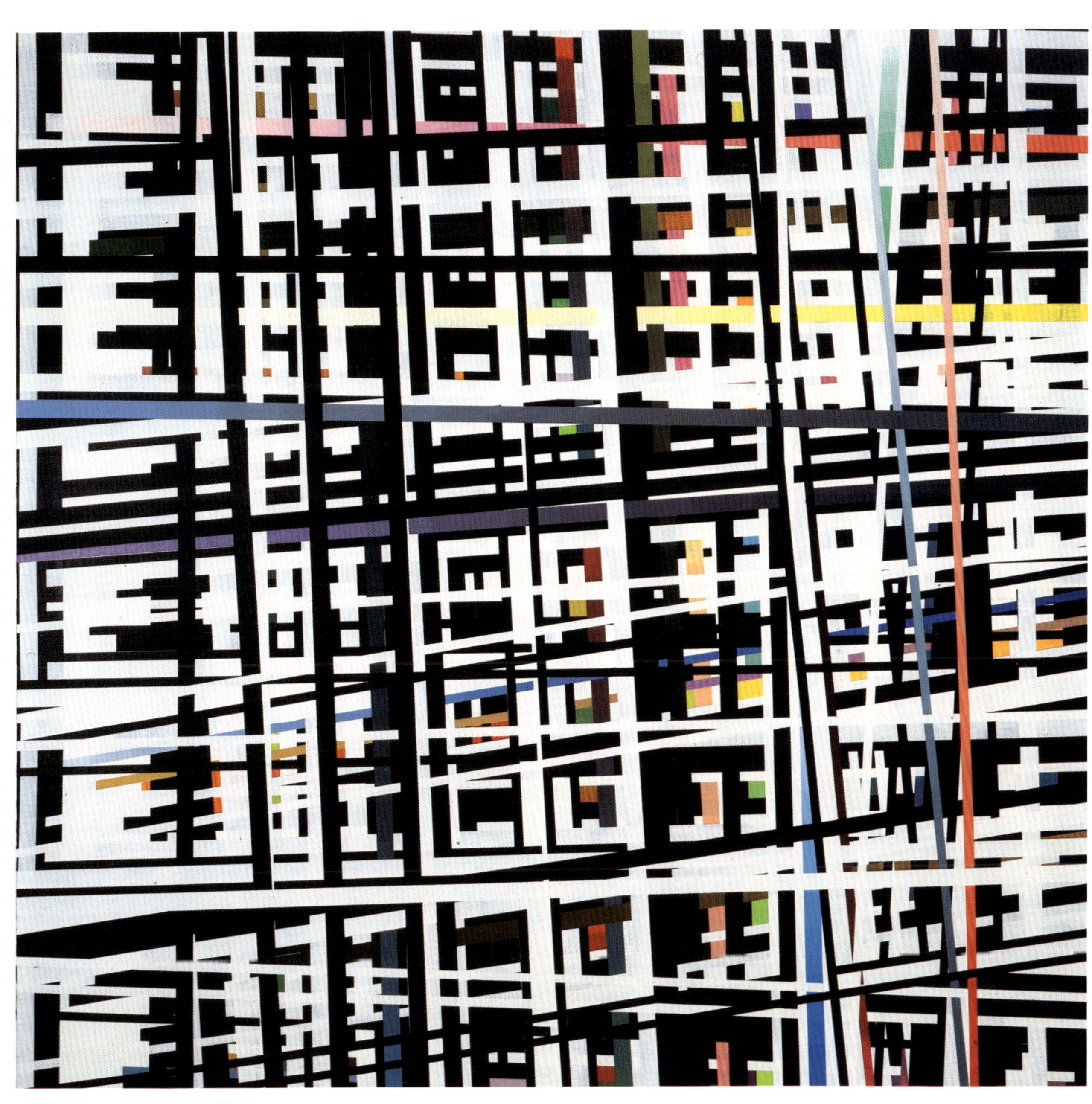

19 *American*, 1994
    acrylic on canvas
    96 × 96 inches

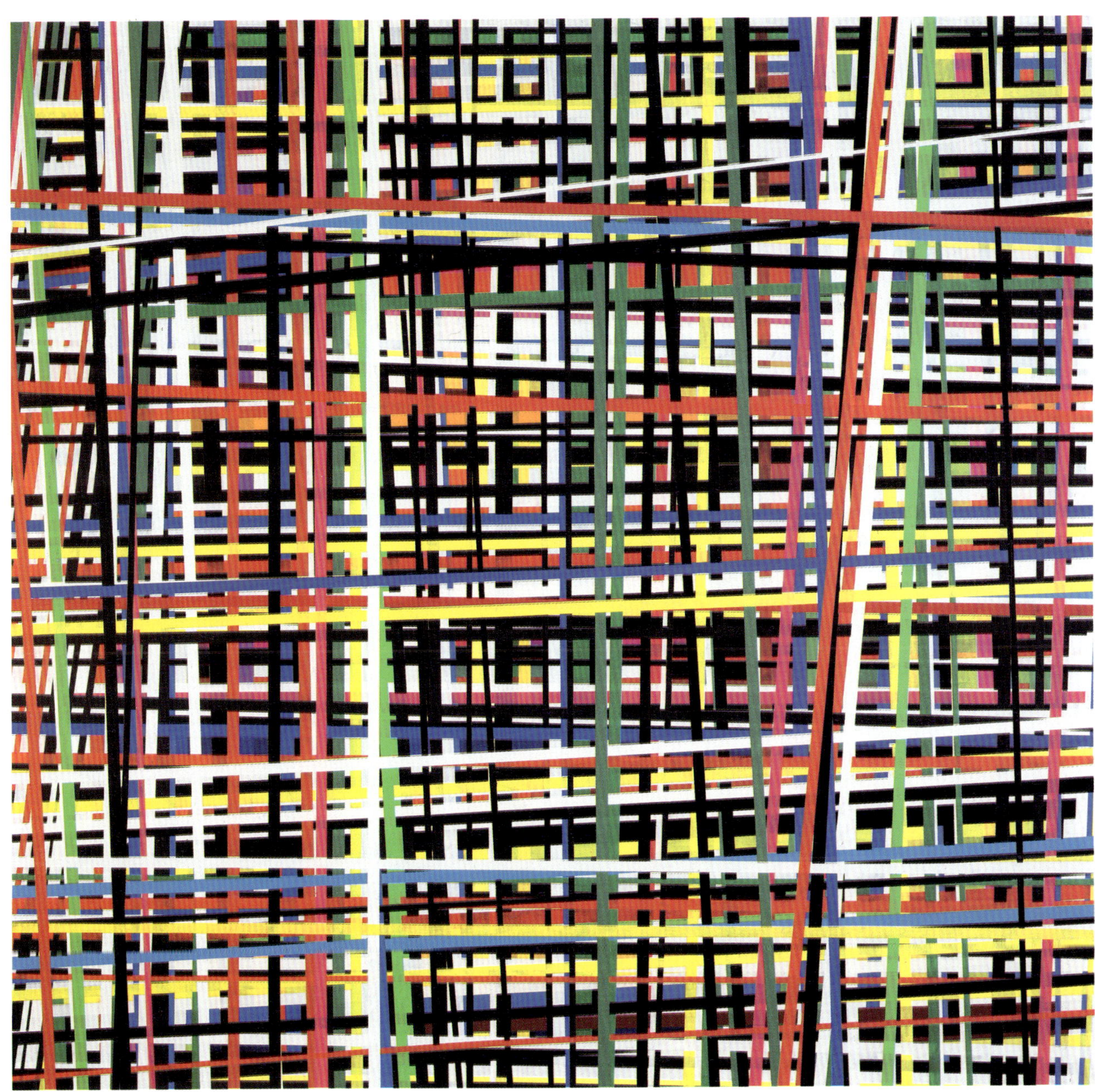

20 *Mirroring a Mutating Moment*, 1991–95
acrylic on canvas
60 × 60 inches

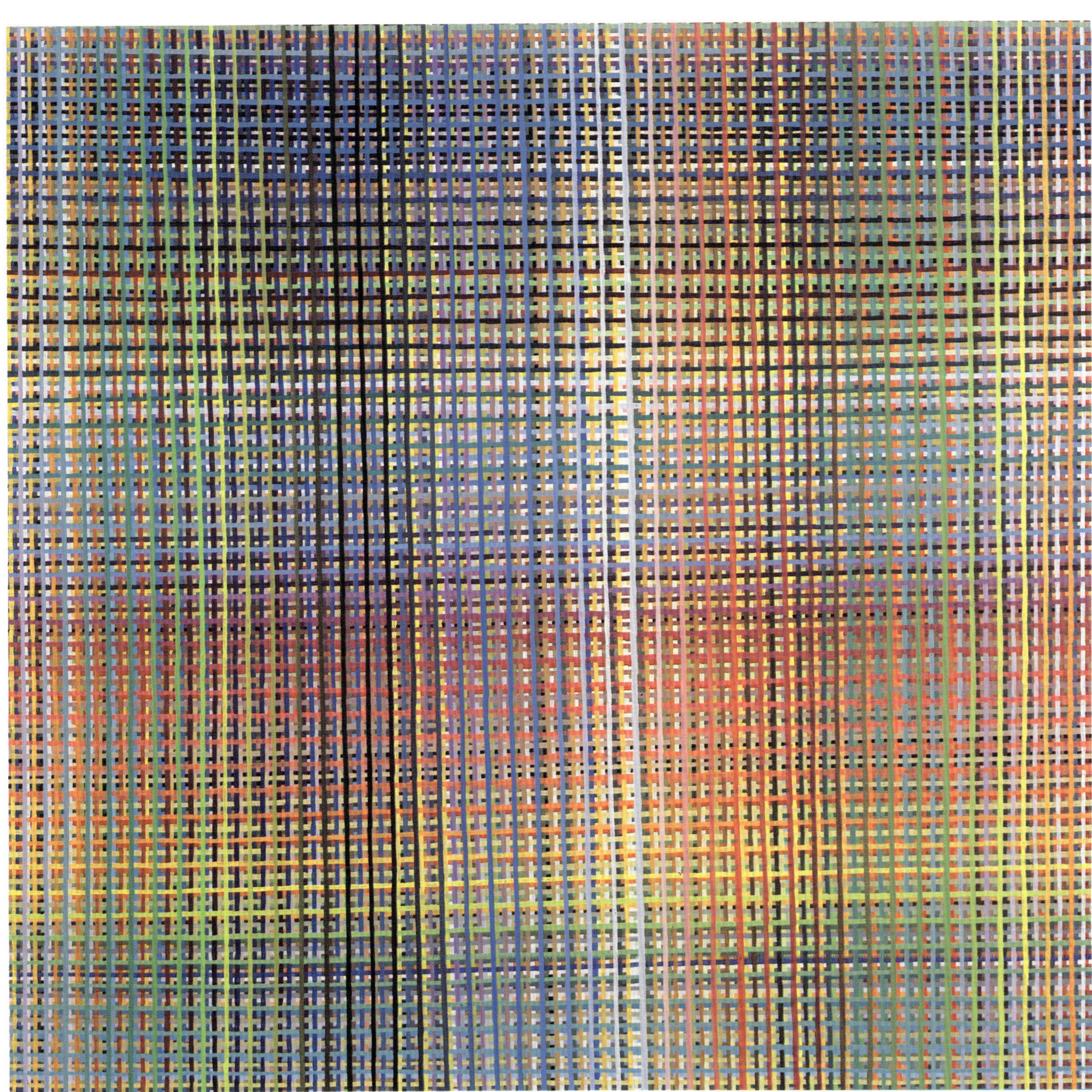

21 *Conquering*, 1995
acrylic on canvas
108 × 72 inches

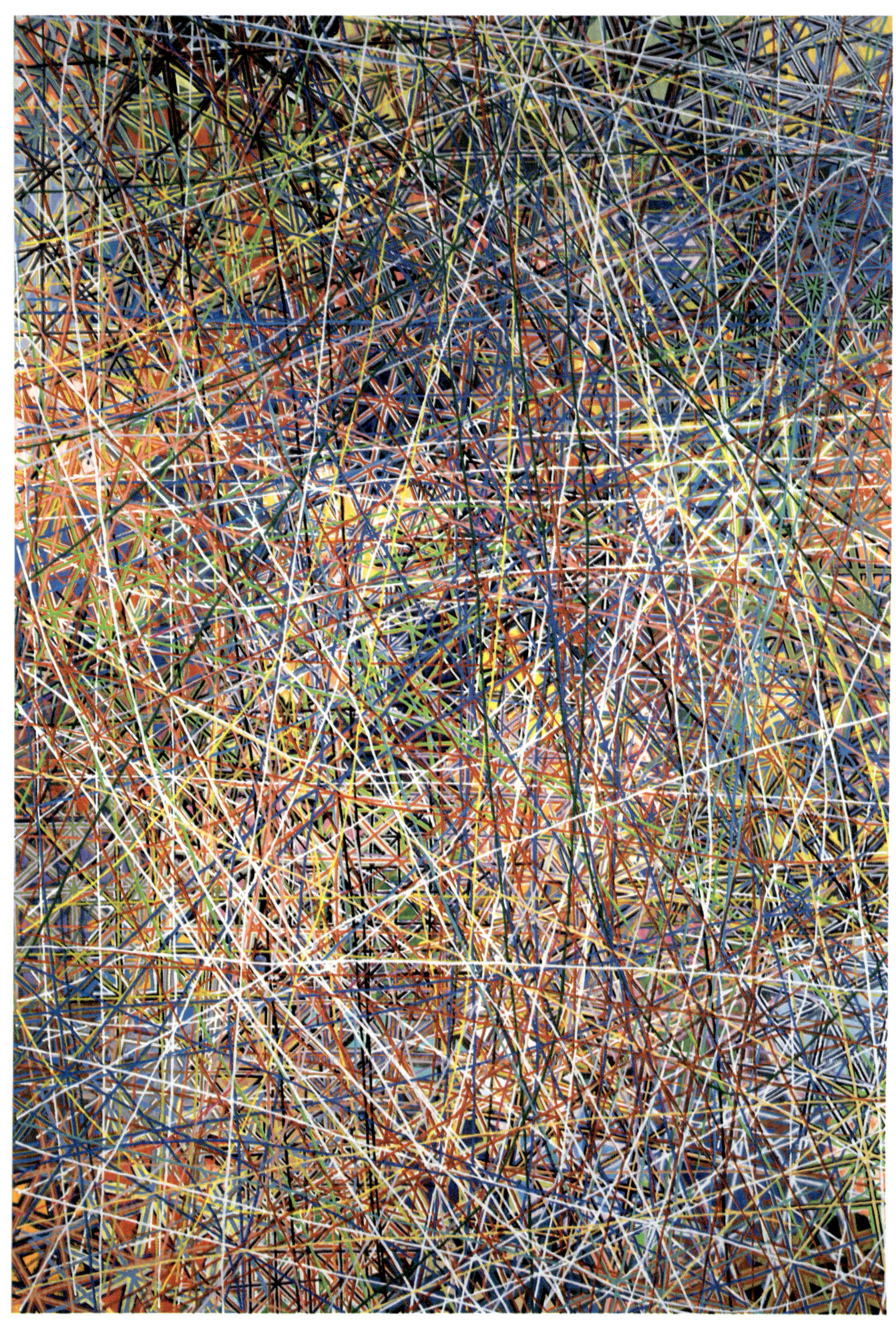

22 *Dream Twister #4 (Testimonial)*, 1996
acrylic on canvas
60 × 60 inches

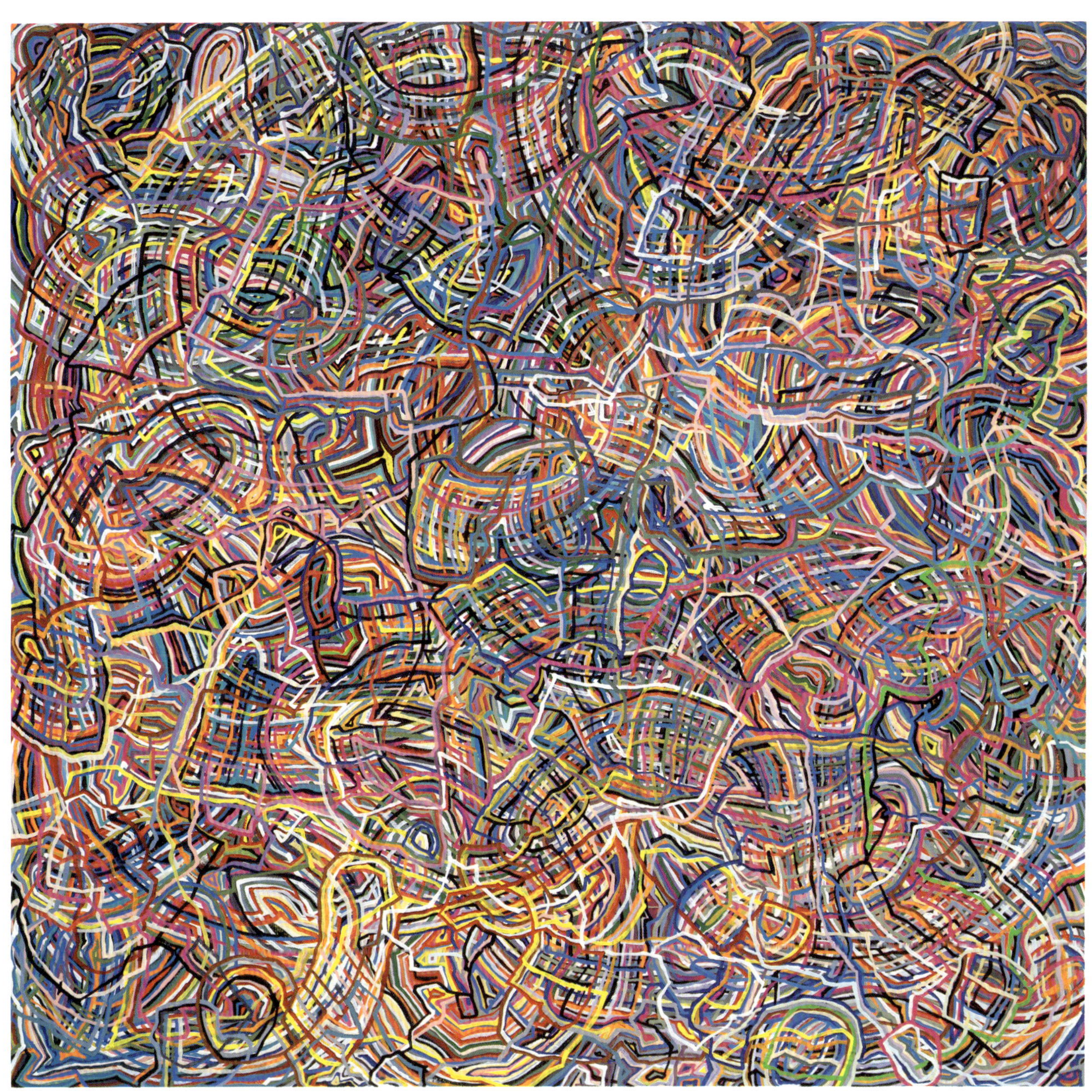

23 *Grand Circle,* 1997
    acrylic on canvas
    113 inches diameter

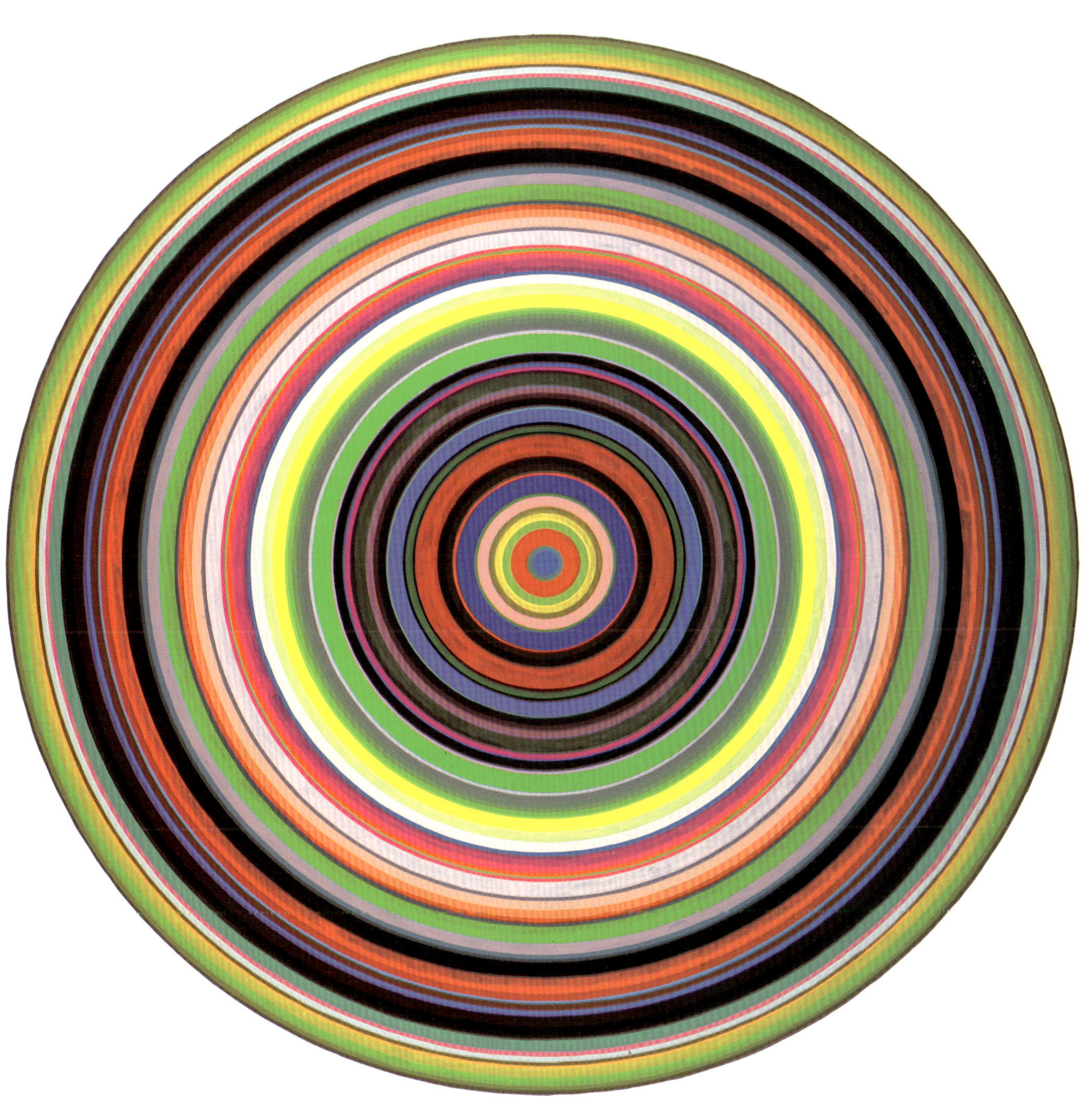

24 *Arsenal of Stars for Chance*, 1997
acrylic on canvas
96 × 96 inches

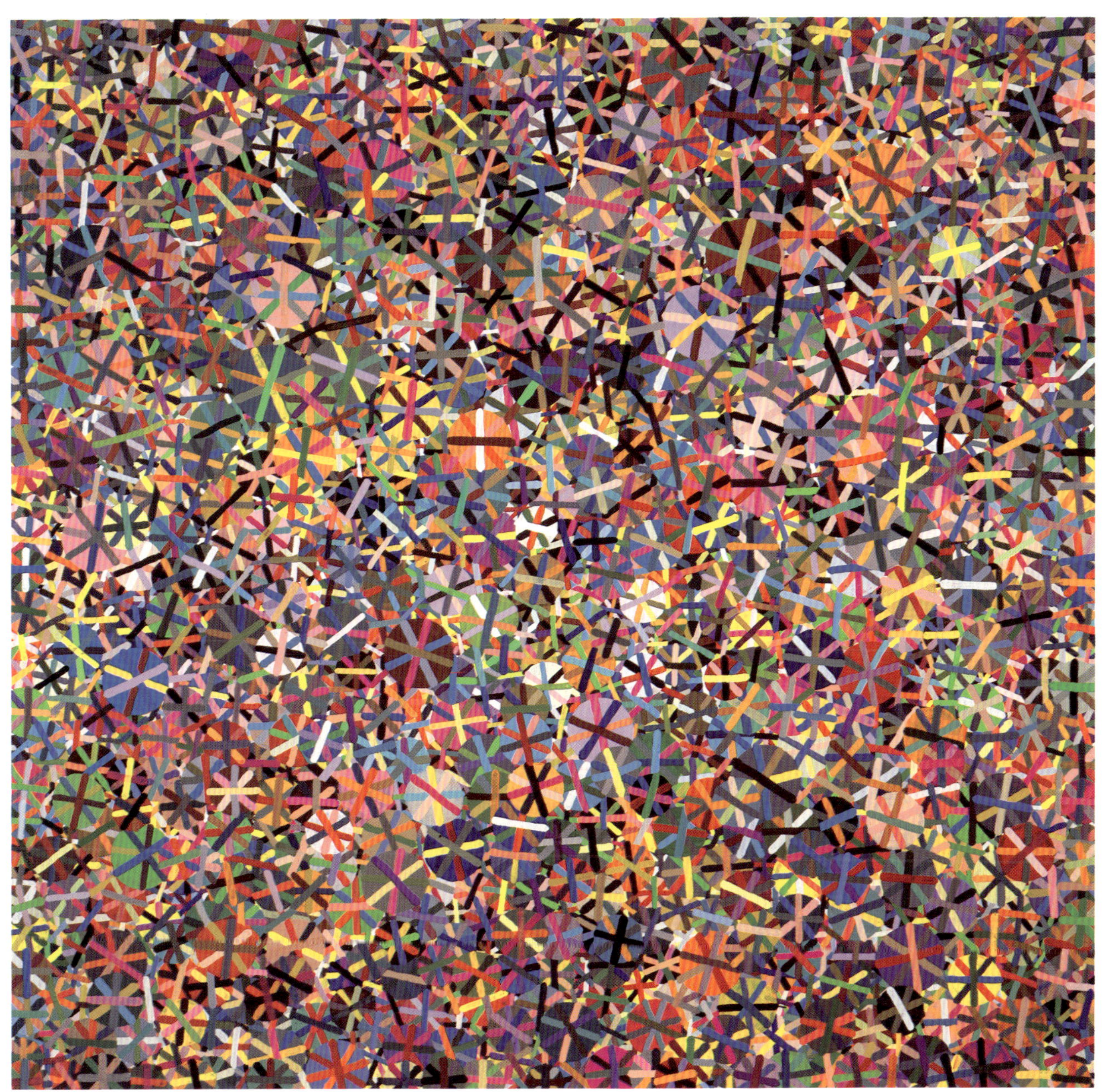

CHECKLIST OF THE EXHIBITION

All dimensions are given in inches; height precedes
width precedes depth.

Barcelona Painting, 1975
acrylic on canvas
40 × 13

Weapon, 1980
enamel, monofilament, and aluminum
11 × 4 × 4
Collection of Bill Ritter and Janny Scott,
       New York City

Weapon, 1980
aluminum and rubber
13 × 4 × 4

Spear, 1981
wood, acrylic paint, and rhinestones
70 × 6 × 6
Collection of Natasha Sigmund, New York City

Dried in Sound, 1981
oil and acrylic on canvas
84 × 58

Isn't It Wonderful, 1981
oil and acrylic on canvas
17 × 9 ¾

Bullet, 1982
lacquer on wood
17 × 5¼ × 5¼

Urn, 1982
acrylic, tape, and wood
29 × 18 × 18

EE2, 1982
acrylic on bamboo and wood
142 × 13 × 13
Collection of Joseph Austin,
       Manhattan Beach, California

The Loss Promotes the Gain, 1983
paper and staples (aggraphage)
size and elements variable

Night Life, 1987
acrylic on canvas
96 × 72

Untitled, 1987
acrylic on canvas
36 × 8
Collection of Tom Rosenberg, Chicago

Foo Lion, 1987
acrylic and wood
44 × 32 × 30
Private Collection, New York City

Fez, 1988–89
acrylic on canvas
43 × 43
Collection of Rebecca and Alex Trepte,
       La Jolla, California

Full Circle, 1990
acrylic on canvas
84 diameter

Night Light, 1990
acrylic on canvas
72 × 60
Collection of Ruth Pastine, New York City

Mirror #33, 1991
acrylic on canvas
60 × 60
The Maslow Collection, Wilkes-Barre, Pennsylvania

Prayers, 1991
acrylic on canvas
60 diameter

Black and White Mirror, Disappearing, 1992
acrylic on panel
14 × 11
Collection of Gwenolee and Bernard Zürcher, Paris

Ruth's Truths, 1993
acrylic on canvas
60 × 60
Collection of Thompson Publishing Group, Washington, DC

Processing Funk and Wonder #2, 1994
acrylic on canvas
63 × 63
Collection of John B. Koegel, New York City

Conquering, 1995
acrylic on canvas
108 × 72
Courtesy Quint Contemporary Art, La Jolla, California

Dream Twister #4 (Testimonial), 1996
acrylic on canvas
60 × 60
Courtesy Galerie Zürcher, Paris

Mulholland Palette for T.L., 1997
acrylic on canvas
12 × 12
Courtesy Brian Gross Fine Art, San Francisco

Grand Circle, 1997
acrylic on canvas
113 diameter

Arsenal of Stars for Chance, 1997
acrylic on canvas
96 × 96

A NOTE ON THE ILLUSTRATIONS

Several important paintings shown in this catalogue could not be included in the exhibition. In addition to *Mirroring Heart (Banding)*, collection of the artist, shown on the cover, they include the following:

Figure 7, Collection Angelika and Marco Vianello-Chiodo, London
Figure 10, Collection of the artist
Figure 12, Collection of Ralph Wernicke, Stuttgart, Germany
Figure 16, Courtesy Galerie Zürcher, Paris
Figure 19, Private Collection, San Juan, Puerto Rico
Figure 20, Private Collection, Paris

GARY LANG

Born: Los Angeles, 1950
Resides: New York City

EDUCATION

Chouinard Art Institute, Los Angeles, 1968–1969
Whitney Museum of American Art, Independent Study
Program, 1970–1971
California Institute of the Arts, Valencia (B.F.A., 1973)
Yale University, New Haven (M.F.A., 1975)

AWARDS AND HONORS

The Elizabeth Foundation for the Arts Grant, 1995
Fulbright/Hayes Travel Grant, Barcelona, Spain, 1975–1977
N.E.A. Yale University, Sculpture Commission, 1974

SOLO EXHIBITIONS

1997

Brian Gross Fine Art, San Francisco
Quint Contemporary Art, La Jolla, California
Sordoni Art Gallery, Wilkes University, Wilkes-Barre, Pennsylvania
Galerie Zürcher, Paris

1996

Maud Boreel Fine Art, The Hague, The Netherlands
Crosby Street Project, New York City
Brian Gross Fine Art, San Francisco
Haags Gemeentemuseum, The Hague, The Netherlands

1995

Galerie Zürcher, Paris

1994

Brian Gross Fine Art, San Francisco

1993

Brian Gross Fine Art, San Francisco
Galería Cadaqués, Cadaqués, Spain
Michael Klein Inc., New York City

1992

Michael Klein Inc., New York City
Nina Freudenheim Gallery, Buffalo, New York
Margaret Lipworth Fine Art, Boca Raton, Florida

1991

Annina Nosei Gallery, New York City

1990

Annina Nosei Gallery, New York City
Mark Quint Gallery, La Jolla, California

1989

Simon Watson Gallery, New York City
Annina Nosei Gallery, New York City
Pretto/Berland Hall Gallery, New York City
Mark Quint Gallery, La Jolla, California

1988

Julian Pretto Gallery, New York City

1987

Madison Art Center, Madison, Wisconsin

1986

Mark Quint Gallery, San Diego, California
Galería Cadaqués, Cadaqués, Spain
Kent Gallery, Kent, Connecticut

1984

Kirk de Gooyer Gallery, Los Angeles
Baskerville + Watson Gallery, New York City

1983

Mark Quint Gallery, San Diego
Kirk de Gooyer Gallery, Los Angeles

1982

Downtown Gallery, Los Angeles
Mark Quint Gallery, San Diego

1981

Todd Gallery, Phoenix, Arizona

1980

Ulrike Kantor Gallery, Los Angeles
L.A.C.E. Gallery, Los Angeles

1975

Institute of American Studies, Barcelona, Spain
Centro Cultural de los Estados Unidos, Madrid, Spain

1974

Yale University Art Gallery, New Haven, Connecticut

SELECTED GROUP EXHIBITIONS

1997

Benefit Exhibition, Pat Hearn Gallery, New York City
Drawing From Life, Stark Gallery, New York City
*Gramercy International Contemporary Art Fair Miami at the Raleigh
  Hotel*, Friedman-Guinness, Miami, Florida
Gramercy International Contemporary Art Fair at Chateau Marmont,
  Friedman-Guinness, Los Angeles
FIAC, Paris

1996

Gramercy International Contemporary Art Fair at Chateau Marmont,
  Friedman-Guinness, Los Angeles
The Collection of Julian Pretto, Wadsworth Atheneum,
  Hartford, Connecticut
Mid-Winter Exhibition, Brian Gross Fine Art, San Francisco
Quint Contemporary Art, La Jolla, California

1995

Color Painting, Brian Gross Fine Art, San Francisco
Julian's Show, Littlejohn Contemporary, New York City
Arresting Images, Gallery 400, The University of Illinois at Chicago

1994

New York City Abstract Painting, Salvatore Ala Gallery,
  New York City
About Color, Charles Cowles Gallery, New York City
Géométrie en Question, Galerie Zürcher, Paris

1993

The Return of the Cadavre Exquis, The Drawing Center,
New York City
Three Painters, Margaret Lipworth Fine Art,
Boca Raton, Florida
East Coast-West Coast, Nancy Drysdale Gallery, Washington, DC
Sailing to Byzantium with Disenchantment, Sergio Tossi Arte
Contemporanea, Prato, Italy
Collage, Brian Gross Fine Art, San Francisco
Lang, McLaughlin, Venezia, Nina Freudenheim Gallery,
Buffalo, New York
Kurswechsel, Michael Klein Inc. at Transart Exhibitions,
Cologne, Germany

1992

Ecstacy, Dooley Le Cappelaine, New York City
Geometric Strategies, Marilyn Pearl Gallery, New York City
Ageometry, Michael Klein Inc., New York City
Vibology, White Columns, New York City

1991

Annina Nosei Gallery, New York City
Summer Show, Michael Klein Inc., New York City
Nancy Drysdale Gallery, Washington, DC
Hill Gallery, Birmingham, Michigan
Preview, Michael Klein Inc., New York City

1990

Annina Nosei Gallery, New York City
Grids, Vrej Baghoomian Gallery, New York City
The Grid, Ben Shahn Galleries, William Paterson College,
Wayne, New Jersey
Mark Quint Gallery, La Jolla, California
Fluid Geometry, Cummings Art Center, Connecticut College,
New London, Connecticut
Group Exhibition, Guillen & Tresserra Galería d'Art, Barcelona

1989

Artists of the 80s: Selected Works from the Maslow Collection, Sordoni
Art Gallery, Wilkes College, Wilkes-Barre, Pennsylvania
Aspects of Painting, Julian Pretto Gallery, New York City
Invitational, Fiction/Non-Fiction Gallery, New York City
Group Exhibition, Annina Nosei Gallery, New York City
Coming of Age, Madison Art Center, Madison, Wisconsin

1988

Mutations, Annina Nosei Gallery, New York City
Albright-Knox Museum, Buffalo, New York
Julian Pretto Gallery, New York City
Adler Gallery, Los Angeles
Small Format, Lang and O'Hara, New York City

1987

Adler Gallery, Los Angeles
Working in Brooklyn—Painting, Brooklyn Museum,
Brooklyn, New York

1986

Paris Biennale, Paris
Adler Gallery, Los Angeles
Modern Objects: A New Dawn, Baskerville + Watson, New York City

1985

Off the Streets, Los Angeles
Metropolitan Transit, Los Angeles
Bill and Merry Norris Collection, Pepperdine University,
Los Angeles
Recent Painting in Southern California, Fisher Gallery, University of
Southern California, Los Angeles

1984

Crime and Punishment, Triton Museum, Santa Clara, California
A Broad Spectrum: Contemporary Los Angeles Painters and Sculptors,
Design Center, Los Angeles
Olympiad: Summer '84, Koplin Center, Los Angeles

1983

University Place Gallery, New York City
L.A.C.E. Gallery, Los Angeles
Jan Baum Gallery, Los Angeles
Plains Museum of Art, Moorhead, Minnesota
Group Exhibition, Mark Quint Gallery, San Diego

1982

4th Anniversary of Chinese Chance, University Place Gallery,
New York City
Sunday in Rio, L.A.C.E., Los Angeles
Theatrical Abstractions, Jan Baum Gallery, Los Angeles
Sanders Collection, Plains Art Museum, Moorhead, Minnesota

1981

Group Exhibition, Molly Barnes Gallery, Los Angeles
Intimate Object, Downtown Gallery, Los Angeles
Emerging Downtown Los Angeles Artists, Cyprus Gallery,
    Los Angeles
California Artists, Tower Gallery, New York City
Wall Constructions, Security Pacific Bank, Los Angeles
Ulrike Kantor, Los Angeles
Gary Lang and Joe Fay, Mark Quint Gallery, Los Angeles
The New Art of Downtown Los Angeles, Madison Art Center, Madison,
    Wisconsin (traveled to four North American cities)
Recent Acquisitions, Community Redevelopment Agency,
    Los Angeles

1978

United Nations Plaza, New York City

1976

Ed Thorp Gallery, New York City

1975

Americans Painting in Spain, Institute of North American Studies,
    Barcelona (traveled to Madrid)
Group Exhibition, Geneva

1973

Yale University Art Gallery, New Haven, Connecticut

1972

Whitney Museum of American Art, New York City

SELECTED LITERATURE

Bacon, George. "Un tour des galeries," *Le Journal des Arts*
    (September 1994): 41.
Blain, Michael. "Formalist Ammunition," *Los Angeles Times*
    (December 30, 1980).
Brenson, Michael. "Art: Brooklyn Painters," *The New York Times*
    (July 3, 1987): III, 23.
Camper, Fred. "Taking Aim at Weapons," *Chicago Reader*
    (September 15, 1995): 34–35.
Davis, Phil. "Point of Departure," *Isthmus* [Madison, Wiscon-
    sin] (June 5, 1987): 26.

Farmer, Rob. "Art in the Round: The Sensational Circles of
    New York Artist Gary Lang," *Where San Francisco* (June
    1996): 51.
Goldman, Leah. "San Diego/Gary Lang/Mark Quint," *Art
    News* (December 1986): 27–28.
Hawkins, Julie. "The Circle Game," *San Francisco Chronicle* (May
    5, 1996): 17.
Hicks, Emily. "Things Fall Apart," *Artweek* (August, 25,
    1984): 6.
Huntington, Richard. "Art," *The Buffalo News* (September 10,
    1993): 20.
———. "Beauty's Truth," *The Buffalo News* (September 10,
    1993).
———. "Titled Eye," *The Buffalo News* (June 12, 1992): 35.
———. "Ugly Beauty," *The Buffalo News* (October 1, 1993):
    24.
Huser, France. "L'Amérique à Paris," *L'Officiel de la Mode*
    (November 1994): 202–204.
Jolis, Alan. "In Brief: Gary Lang: Zurcher, Paris," *Art News*
    (January 1996): 135.
Kaiser, Franz W. *Gary Lang: The Hague Project* (The Hague: Haags
    Gemeentemuseum, 1996), exhibition catalogue.
Koplos, Janet. "Gary Lang at Crosby Street Project," *Art in
    America* (September 1996): 108–109.
Larsen, Susan C. "Gary Lang at Mark Quint Gallery," *Artforum*
    (September 1982): 84–85.
———. *Sunshine and Shadow: Recent Painting in Southern California*
    (Los Angeles: The Fellows of Contemporary Art,
    1985), exhibition catalogue.
McDonald, Robert. "Paintings That Defy Description," *Los
    Angeles Times* (October 1, 1986): 1, 7.
———. "Portraits of the Artist As Life Itself," *Visions*
    (Winter 1993): 31–32.
Moorman, Margaret. "Gary Lang at Annina Nosei," *Art News*
    (December 1988): 206, 210.
Morgan, Robert C. "Three Strategies," *Art Press* (February-
    March, 1996): 64–65.
Nathan, Jean. "Gary Lang," (New York: Michael Klein Inc.,
    1991), exhibition brochure.
Norklun, K. "The Disjunctive Experience," *Artweek* (February
    19, 1983): 6.
Nuridsany, Michel. "Gary Lang," *Figaro* (September 19,
    1995).

Ohlman, Leah. "San Diego/Gary Lang/Mark Quint," *Art News* (December 1986): 27–28.

Ostrow, Saul. "Gary Lang Interview," *BOMB* 45 (Fall 1993): 14–16.

———. "More Parts to the Whole: Abstract Painting After Modernism," *Art Press* (French Edition, November 1995).

O'Toole, Judith, H. *Artists of the 80s: Selected Works from the Maslow Collection* (Wilkes-Barre, Pennsylvania: Sordoni Art Gallery, Wilkes College, 1989), exhibition catalogue.

P., R.L. [Pincus, Robert, L.] "Galleries Downtown," *Los Angeles Times* (August 10, 1984): VI, 16.

Pincus, Robert, L. "Art of Excess: On Energy Alone Lang's Canvases Hit the Bulls'-eye," *The San Diego Union-Tribune* (March 20, 1997): 40.

———. "Mark Quint Finds Space for New Art," *The San Diego Union* (October 1, 1989): E-3.

P., J.L. [Pinte, Jean-Louis] "A Vibrant Geometry," *Figaroscope* (September 28, 1994,): 54.

Pinte, Jean-Louis. "Gary Lang: Les miroirs de l'âme," *Figaroscope* (October 4–10, 1995): 43.

Rubinstein, Raphael. "Gary Lang at Michael Klein," *Art in America* (March 1994): 96–97.

Saltz, Jerry. "A Year in the Life: Tropic of Painting," *Art in America* (October 1994): 90–101.

Scott, Sue. "Ageometry," *Art News* (May 1993):141–142.

Selwyn, Marc. "Three Painters," *Flash Art* (November-December 1989): 126–127.

Smith, Roberta. "Gary Lang: 'Hague Project,'" *The New York Times* (February 9, 1996): C23.

———. "Old, Traditional and Alternative Spaces," *The New York Times* (May 5, 1989): III, 30.

Stamets, Bill. "Art: A Warm Gun; A Wet Paintbrush," *Chicago Sunday Times* (September 29, 1995): NC 3.

Stockinger, Jacob. "Color Shows Joy, Tension of the Artist," *The Capital Times* [Madison, Wisconsin] (June 12, 1987): 36.

[Tomkins, Calvin]. "Ageometry," *The New Yorker* (December 28, 1992): 35.

Vezin, Luc, and Bernard Zürcher. "La FIAC (et le marché de l'art?)," *InfoMatin* (October 7 & 8, 1994): 26.

Wat, Pierre. "Gary Lang: L'Intuitif," *Beaux Arts* (October 1995): 53.

Westfall, Stephen. "Gary Lang at Julian Pretto," *Art in America* (December 1988): 146.

———. "Gary Lang: A Conversation with Stephen Westfall," *Tema Celeste* (January/March 1992): 98–99.

———. *Fluid Geometry* (New London: Cummings Art Center, Connecticut College, 1990), exhibition catalogue.

Zimmer, William. "Fluid Geometry: Six Painters Offer Expressionistic Shapes," *The New York Times* (December 9, 1990): XII.

Zinsser, John. "Geometry and Its Discontents," *Tema Celeste* (Autumn 1991): 72–76.

SELECTED PUBLIC COLLECTIONS

A. T. & T., Somerset, New Jersey
The Brooklyn Museum
City Redevelopment Agency, Los Angeles
Contemporary Art Museum, University of South Florida, Tampa
The Detroit Institute of Arts
IBM Corporation, Somers, New York
Madison Art Center, Madison, Wisconsin
The Maslow Collection, Wilkes-Barre, Pennsylvania
Meadowbrook Art Gallery, Oakland University, Rochester, Michigan
Museum of Art, University of Michigan, Ann Arbor
Nordstern, Cologne, Germany
Paine Webber, New York City
Plains Art Museum, Moorhead, Minnesota
Portland Museum of Art, Portland, Maine
Rayovac, Madison, Wisconsin
Thompson Publishing Group, New York City
Tuttle & Taylor, Los Angeles
Wadsworth Atheneum, Hartford, Connecticut

EXHIBITION UNDERWRITERS

Diversified Records Services, Inc.
Annette Evans Foundation for the
        Arts and Humanities
Franklin First Savings Bank
Friends of the Sordoni Art Gallery
Maslow Lumia Bartorillo Advertising, Inc.
Mellon Bank, N.A.
Pennsylvania Council on the Arts
The John Sloan Memorial Foundation, Inc.
Andrew J. Sordoni, III
Wilkes University

SPONSORS

The Business Council
CBI-Creative Business Interiors
Eastern Insurance Group
Friedman Electric Supply Co., Inc.
Marquis Art and Frame
Nabisco, Inc.
G. R. Noto Electrical Construction
Panzitta Enterprises, Inc.
Pennsylvania Millers Mutual Insurance Co.
Rosenn, Jenkins and Greenwald, L.L.P.
Trion Industries Inc.

This exhibition is in honor of Dr. Roy E. Morgan and has
been funded in part by a generous gift from the Sordoni
Foundation. Maslow Lumia Bartorillo Advertising, Inc.
provided additional support to underwrite the catalogue.

ACKNOWLEDGMENTS

This exhibition and catalogue would not have been
possible without the enthusiastic support of Gary Lang.

Additional thanks to the following:
Joseph Austin
John Beck
Marsha Chase
Eric Fischl
Esther Friedman
Thomas H. Garver
Ap Gewald
Brian Gross
Robert J. Heaman, Ph.D.
Franz W. Kaiser
John B. Koegel
Nancy L. Krueger
Raymond and Shirley Lang
Susan C. Larsen, Ph.D.
Melanie Maslow Lumia
The Maslow Collection
Ruth Pastine
Mark Quint
Bill Ritter
Tom Rosenberg
Jon Schaffer
Robert Schweitzer
Janny Scott
Natasha Sigmund
Andrew J. Sordoni, III
Eric Stark
Richard E. Thompson
Rebecca and Alex Trepte
James Turrell
Jeff Wecker
Gwenolee and Bernard Zürcher

ADVISORY COMMISSION

Freddie Bittenbender
Christopher N. Breiseth, Ph.D.
Marion M. Conyngham
Virginia C. Davis, Chair
Stanley I Grand, Ph.D.
Robert J. Heaman, Ph.D.
Mary Jane Henry
Keith A. Hunter, Esq.
J. Michael Lennon, Ph.D.
Melanie Maslow Lumia
Theo Lumia
Kenneth Marquis
Constance R. McCole
Hank O'Neal
Arnold Rifkin
Kim Ross
Charles A. Shaffer, Esq.
Susan Shoemaker, Esq.
William Shull
Helen Farr Sloan
Andrew J. Sordoni, III
Sally Sprankle
Sanford B. Sternlieb, M.D.
Mindi Thalenfeld
Thomas H. van Arsdale
Joel Zitofsky

STAFF

Stanley I Grand, Ph.D., *Director*
Nancy L. Krueger, *Co-ordinator*
Earl W. Lehman, *Preparator*

Gallery Attendants
Tom Harrington
Sarah Karlavage
Amy Mazeitis
Lisa Tabbit